DUNCAN OF LIVERPOOL

WILLIAM HENRY DUNCAN, M.D.
Medical Officer of Health, Liverpool, 1847–1863

DUNCAN OF LIVERPOOL

Being an account of the work of
Dr W. H. Duncan
Medical Officer of Health of Liverpool
1847–63

BY

W. M. Frazer

O.B.E., M.D., M.Sc., D.P.H.,

OF GRAY'S INN, BARRISTER-AT-LAW

Professor of Hygiene, University of Liverpool
Medical Officer of Health, City and Port of Liverpool

Carnegie Publishing, 1997

First published in 1947 by Hamish Hamilton Medical Books
90 Great Russell Street, London WC1.

This edition, with a foreword by John Ashton,
published by Carnegie Publishing Ltd, 18 Maynard Street,
Preston, Lancashire PR2 2AL

British Library Cataloguing-in-Publication Data
A catalogue record for this book is available
from the British Library

ISBN 1-85936-055-6

Printed in the UK by Bookcraft (Bath) Ltd

FOREWORD
John Ashton

Dr William M. Frazer was the sixth Medical Officer of Health for Liverpool (1931–1953). Since then there have been four more: Professor Andrew Semple, Duncan Doulton, June Phillips and Ruth Hussey. In 1974, following local government reorganisation, the Liverpool tradition of the Medical Officer of Health being also the University of Liverpool Professor of Public Health came to an end and the Medical Officer of Health in the local authority was replaced by a community physician based in the health authority. There was in effect a peculiar period in the late '70s and early '80s when Public Health was replaced by the vague and misunderstood term of Community Medicine to be practised by community physicians. In my view this misguided move came about as a result of a loss of confidence and direction and a form of false consciousness which held that the future lay in a close relationship with clinicians rather than with the broad coalition of those who have an impact on public health, including clinicians. It is worth remembering that Duncan himself, although a founder of the medical school in Liverpool, was very much an environmentalist, first and foremost, and very much a practitioner of the political arts.

This aberrant period of community medicine was seen off by the Acheson report on Public Health in England in 1988 when the Director of Public Health (based still in the Health Authority) made her entrance and when the tradition of annual reports on the health of the population, first introduced by Duncan re-appeared after an absence of fourteen years.

Nineteen-ninety-seven is not only the sesquicent-ennial year of public health in Liverpool but is also the centenary of the University of Liverpool Department of Public Health, making it one of the earliest academic centres to teach this discipline. Trinity College, Dublin, was first in 1871, closely followed by Cambridge in 1875. In 100 years the Liverpool Chair of Public Health has only been held by four incumbants. Hope (1897–1931), Frazer (1933–1953), Semple (1953–1974) and Pharoah (1979–1997).

Of these four Frazer turned out to be not only an enduring and effective Medical Officer of Health but in addition was no mean historian. This little book which was first published in 1947 on the centenary of Duncan's appointment, is packed full of fascinating detail of the challenges which faced Duncan and his colleagues, Thomas Fresh, the Inspector of Nuisances and James Newlands, the Borough Engineer. It is brought to life both by the crisp style and the delightful vignettes and anecdotes. The history of public health in Liverpool is one of alliances of the most effective kind (some might say almost cabals). Duncan, New-lands and Fresh was one such partnership, but a later one was that of Professor Andrew Semple, Brian Meredith Davies (a public health physician who was also Director of Social Services in Liverpool after 1974) and Tom Hobday, a university lecturer, public health physician, barrister, Tory councillor and chairman of the City Health Committee. When I took over Tom's position at the University of Liverpool in 1983 it was he who introduced me to Frazer's book (and to an invaluable network in public health, although we were poles apart politically). Frazer's book was at that time out of print but by good fortune and the willing help of Mrs Joyce Clark of 'Worm Books' of Conway Road in London, I was able to track down the remaining stock from 1947. It is this stock which has so far enabled us to present a mint condition copy to each Duncan Lecturer since 1983 as well as to a select number of practitioners globally whose contributions have merited this accolade! However the stock is low and cannot last for ever, and with the renaissance of public health at a local, national and international level, there is an increasing demand for copies based on a desire to learn past lessons and derive inspiration.

So in 1997, 150 years on from Duncan taking up his appointment as recommended by Chadwick 'That for the general promotion of the means necessary to prevent disease it would be good economy to appoint a district medical officer independent of private practice, and with the securities of special qualifications and responsibilities to initiate sanitary measures, and reclaim the execution of the law', it seems the right time to go to press again. It is also apposite that in the 150th anniversary year of the appointment of the country's first MOH, we now have the country's first Minister of Public Health. May you find much nourishment, guidance and inspiration from these pages!

John Ashton
Regional Director of Public Health
May 1997

ACKNOWLEDGEMENT

The publishers would like to thank Hamish Hamilton for allowing us to publish this important little book. Our thanks also go to John Ashton, whose idea it was, and to Sally Sheard, who helped make it happen.

PREFACE

THE purpose behind the writing of this small book is to commemorate the centenary of the appointment of the first Medical Officer of Health in the person of Dr. W. H. Duncan, of Liverpool. It may be appropriate that one of Duncan's successors should write an account of his official life, and, so far as I am aware, this is the first biography of a Medical Officer of Health to be written at all.

Duncan's life was an unpretentious one; there were no high-lights in it, and no important or spectacular events occurred to add excitement to these pages in which it is recorded. The justification for writing an account of his official career seems to me to be, first, that he was a pioneer in the practice of sanitation as applied to the problems of a large and rapidly growing town, and, secondly, that he was the first Medical Officer of Health to be appointed in this country. The honour of making the first appointment of this kind rests with Liverpool and it is to the eternal credit of the men who governed the borough in those days just before the middle of the nineteenth century that they so quickly perceived the evils happening in their midst and so soon took action to remedy them.

Owing to the scantiness of the official records of that time it has been impossible to follow many of the matters mentioned in the text to their administrative conclusion. There were no typewriters and no filing systems, and except for documents such as annual and special reports, and Duncan's letter-books, to which extensive reference has been made, there are no departmental records now available. Fortunately, the epidemics which occurred during each of the years 1847, 1849 and 1854 are well documented in the

annual reports and in the Medical Officer of Health's
letters to the General Board of Health.

In 1947 the post of Medical Officer of Health will
have reached the respectable age—for a local government appointment—of a hundred years, and during
that period many changes have taken place, all tending
to increase the duties and responsibilities attaching to
the office. Until the beginning of the twentieth century
the functions of the Medical Officer of Health were
almost entirely concerned with what may be broadly
referred to as sanitation—infectious diseases, housing,
nuisances, lodging-houses, and the inspection of food;
but after the turn of the century a whole field of new
activities opened up, adding to the Health Department's
duties, as the years went by, the supervision of mid-
wives, the medical inspection and treatment of school
children, the administration of schemes for the diagnosis
and treatment of venereal diseases and the care of the
mother and the young child. The last of the three stages
into which this period may be divided was ushered in
by the Local Government Act, 1929, whereby hospitals
and certain other services were transferred from the
Boards of Guardians to the councils of counties and
county boroughs. Much of this work, including in many
cases the administration of hospitals, became the responsibility of Medical Officers of Health, whose departments reached what was probably their zenith in size
and importance during the period between 1930 and
the outbreak of war in 1939.

Altogether, in the space of a hundred years, there
have been six Medical Officers of Health of Liverpool.
They are: W. H. Duncan (1847–63), W. S. Trench
(1863–77), J. Stopford Taylor (1878–93), E. W. Hope
(1894–1924), A. A. Mussen (1924–31), and the
present writer.

My grateful thanks are due to Professor J. M.
Mackintosh, Dean of the London School of Hygiene
and Tropical Medicine, at whose suggestion this book
was written; to Professor E. W. Hope, O.B.E., for

assistance in connection with the first chapter; to Sir Allen Daley, Medical Officer of Health of the London County Council, for helpful criticisms and advice; to Mr. T. H. Graham, O.B.E., Librarian of the Royal College of Physicians of Edinburgh, for information about Duncan's graduation; and to some of my Liverpool colleagues, especially Mr. W. H. Baines, C.B.E., the Town Clerk, for permission to use some of the Corporation's records; Mr. John Ainsworth, the City Treasurer, for information in regard to officials employed by the Town Council in 1847; and Dr. C. O. Stallybrass and Dr. B. T. J. Glover, of the Liverpool Public Health Department, for reading, and suggesting amendments to, the typescript.

I am also indebted to Miss P. Moore, Sub-Librarian of the Liverpool Athenaeum, for much help in connection with books and records in the Library of that institution; and to Miss M. M. Thompson, of the Liverpool Public Health Department, for her kindness in typing this book during her spare time.

W. M. FRAZER

Liverpool, 1947

CONTENTS

LIST OF ILLUSTRATIONS

DUNCAN OF LIVERPOOL

1

SANITARY CONDITIONS IN LIVERPOOL IN THE EARLY NINETEENTH CENTURY

IT has been said by one of the greatest of English historians that history is a register of the crimes, follies and misfortunes of mankind; but this definition is not, perhaps, all-embracing, and it might be justifiable to claim that included in the record should be the attempts of individual pioneers to undo, or at least to mitigate, the evils which the unwisdom of their fellows has unloosed upon the world. The evils arising so rapidly from the Industrial Revolution in England were all but irremediable, and yet there were men who gained a measure of success in their efforts to improve the lot of the working classes in the manufacturing towns. Some of these pioneers, such as Shaftesbury and Chadwick, worked to establish efficient central administration especially in connection with the Poor Law, while others, such as Duncan in Liverpool, laboured to adapt the local government organization to the sanitary needs of the people. The work of those at the centre was important, but all the recommendations of the various commissions on the health of the labouring classes would have been useless if they had not been brought into effect at the periphery by the devoted labours of sanitary pioneers in the larger towns in the middle years of the last century.

William Henry Duncan was one of these pioneers, and his name is noteworthy in the history of Liverpool partly because, just a century ago, he became the first Medical Officer of Health to hold office in this country, and partly because of his positive achievements in the cause of sanitary reform. He was born in Seel Street, Liverpool, in 1805, the third son and fifth child of George Duncan, a Liverpool merchant. His mother was Christian, the youngest daughter of the Reverend James Currie of Kirkpatrick Fleming, Dumfriesshire. Little is known of his early life and I can obtain no records of it; but he graduated Doctor of Medicine at Edinburgh in 1829 with a thesis entitled *De ventris in reliquum corpus potestate.* His career up to the time when he was appointed Medical Officer of Health of the borough of Liverpool was that of a successful young practitioner. (Furfher details of his appointments are given in Chapter 4.) Early in his professional life he had come into contact with the poverty-stricken denizens of the borough while engaged as a physician to one of the dispensaries, and he appears to have developed strong sympathies with this neglected and downtrodden section of the community. Dr. Duncan collaborated with Mr. (later Sir Edwin) Chadwick in the preparation of Reports on the Condition of the Poor and he gave evidence on this subject before a Select Committee of the House of Commons.

His early sympathies with the poor and his interest in sanitary reform enhanced the value of his services when they were placed at the disposal of the borough, and enabled him to endure the inevitable failures of the pioneer and the opprobrium which has always been the fate of the reformer.

The borough of Liverpool in which William Henry Duncan was born, and in which he spent the whole of his working life, has a very ancient history which dates from the so-called Charter of King John given on 28th August, 1207. During the following centuries the borough slowly increased in population but until late in the eighteenth century Liverpool was of slight importance as a port, being inferior in that respect to Chester.

In spite of its long history and the favour shown to

it by King John and several of his successors, Liverpool
had only attained to a population of 700 by the year
1565 and the port, as late as 1557, possessed only
thirteen vessels, the largest of which was 100 tons.
The borough, indeed, had to wait until the end of the
seventeenth century for its first period of marked
expansion, which depended, as it did in the nineteenth
century, upon the factories of Lancashire. In the second
half of the seventeenth century the port traded with
Ireland and sent its ships to more distant countries
such as France and Spain and even began to compete
with Hull for some of the Baltic trade. During the
later part of this century it began to trade with America
and the West Indies—a foretaste of the prosperity
which was to come to the borough and port from this
source two hundred years later.

Liverpool's population nevertheless was small until
well on into the nineteenth century. At the 1801 census
its population was 77,653. In 1801 the period of com-
mercial prosperity was at hand and the enormous
expansion of Lancashire's factories brought a large
amount of export and import trade to the port and
determined the character of Liverpool's activities for a
century and a half. With the expansion of trade through
the port came the demand for better facilities for
handling ships, and the gigantic work of constructing
the dock system of Liverpool began. The twenty years
from 1815 to 1835 saw the building of eight new docks,
and others were opened as the century wore on and the
trade of Lancashire with the rest of the world increased.
A race of merchant princes arose out of this prosperity,
and the trade and industry of the borough established
itself as an auxiliary to the needs of the port and of the
commerce passing through it. Banking, insurance,
warehousing and the transport of goods became the
staple industries of Liverpool ministering to the needs
of shipping. These were the main activities and there
were few industries which employed large numbers of
skilled workers. The port itself employed, almost

exclusively, unskilled and casual labour. As a consequence the working-class population of Liverpool contained a large majority of people whose standard of
living was very low and who were exposed to fluctu-
ating periods of unemployment. During the construction of the dock system there was a great inflow of
casual labourers who, when the docks were completed,
remained behind in the borough to swell the ranks of
unskilled workmen who clamoured for employment of
any kind.

This rather unsubstantial prosperity had the far-
reaching consequence that it led to rapid increases in
the population of the borough. The sons of casual
labourers, each generation more numerous than the
last, became casual labourers, suffering in their turn
from unemployment, a low standard of living, and the
effects of insanitary housing. All industrial towns
suffered to some extent from these evils; the tragedy
of Liverpool was that she suffered from them to a far
greater extent than any other large urban area.
Manchester and Birmingham gradually developed
industries and trained armies of skilled workmen, while
Liverpool had only the docks, trades depending upon
the port, and multitudes of casual labourers. The great
increase of population led to an acute housing problem,
and the building trade of the borough was never able
to produce sufficient houses at a price which the casual
labourer was able to pay. This does not mean that few
houses were built in this rapidly expanding borough:
in fact much house building was going on during the
middle years of last century. In a report dated 1867
details are given of the numbers and types of houses
built in Liverpool during the years 1841 to 1866
inclusive. The grand total amounts to 40,661. But only
a small proportion of these were under the value of
£12 per annum and thus suitable for occupation by
persons in the lower income groups. Until 1842 there
were no restrictions on the siting, planning or construction of houses and as a consequence there arose

WIDE COURT CLOSED AT END

in their thousands the court type of house which Duncan so scathingly condemns.

Another vicious type of dwelling was the cellar, which, until the Liverpool Improvement Act of 1842, had not been controlled by any legislation. Liverpool had not only the worst type of cellar dwelling but also a larger proportion of its inhabitants living in cellars than any other town. Moreover, in many parts of the town there was little or no privacy for closet accommodation, and scavenging was very primitive even in the main streets, which were generally paved with rounded boulder stones, their wide interstices serving as reservoirs for filth. Overcrowding was present in an extreme degree; and as the occupations of the low classes of immigrant were uncertain and intermittent, every facility existed for intemperance. Periods of great activity alternated with complete idleness when storm or other conditions made vessels irregular in their arrival.

Meanwhile the Town Council was taking steps to obtain legislative authority to control these conditions and also to supervise the common lodging-houses which were let off to as many occupants as could crowd into them. The land in the districts in which these evils were most pronounced was of a high value, and there was nothing to restrict builders and landlords from the most profitable investment of their money. As a result dwellings were constructed with total disregard of hygienic principles.

The general situation of the labouring classes in Liverpool at that time is described in the words of the census report for 1801:

A large proportion of the population were living in cellars and typhus fever and other diseases carry off many each year in the lower crowded parts of the town. The influx of the labouring classes in search of the means of existence fall victims to disappointment, disease and poverty.

Even disposal of the dead became a public nuisance, whether from burial in churches and chapels or from the custom of opening graves and turning out their contents prematurely to make room for the remains of others; and not infrequently human remains "were in an open public churchyard trampled on and bandied about by a rude rabble for their pastime, the remains being dragged forth to public view and disclosed to the prying eye of a wanton curiosity."[1]

In 1823 a writer (while complimentary to public buildings) says that

> Several of the neighbouring streets present spec-
> tacles of vileness and misery in their lowest forms,
> from which the heart turns in disgust which almost
> overpowers the feeling of commiseration. . . . It is
> deeply to be regretted that dissipation and licentious-
> ness should almost always be the accompaniment of
> extensive commerce and that that valuable character
> —the British sailor—is left to indulgencies which
> destroy the hard-earned wages in orgies of the basest
> description.

We pass on with a glance at what is generally admitted to have been the greatest stimulus to Liverpool's prosperity—the Slave Trade. It must be borne in mind that at no time were cargoes of slaves actually brought to Liverpool.[2] When the trade was at its height it was estimated that Liverpool absorbed five-eighths of the English slave trade, nearly three-sevenths of the whole slave trade of all the European nations, and that the large proportion of Liverpool's shipping so engaged had left Bristol and London far behind as competitors. The round voyage, as it was known,

---

[1] William Moss, *Medical Survey of Liverpool*, London, 1784.

[2] But from time to time small numbers of negro slaves were offered for sale in Liverpool, as in other towns, during the eighteenth century, and advertisements to this effect appeared in the local papers. See *History of the Liverpool Privateers* by Gomer Williams, 1897. Slavery was abolished in the British Isles by the famous decision of Lord Mansfield in Somersett's case (1772) that the status of slavery was unknown to the Common Law of England.

began with a run to West African ports with cargoes readily purchasable by the natives. The next cargo consisted of natives collected and enslaved by the gin-sodden rulers of the neighbouring areas, the middle passage being across to the West Indies or American ports where labour was greatly in demand, and the final stage was the return with the valuable cargo of goods required in this country. "Beyond a doubt," Ramsay Muir remarks, "it was the Slave Trade which raised Liverpool . . . to be one of the richest and most prosperous trading centres in the world."

There can be little doubt that many people financially interested in the African trade, as it was called, were ignorant of the true state of affairs. But, as J. B. Russell said in connection with bad housing: "To plead ignorance is to plead guilty."

One of the strangest of all men found in such an association was the Rev. John Newton, best known as the friend of Cowper and the author of "How Sweet the Name of Jesus sounds" and other hymns. These characteristics in Newton evidently developed after adventures in his earlier life as a midshipman in the navy.

To realize the measure of Duncan's services to Liverpool one must describe briefly not only the conditions of the borough as he found them but the preceding circumstances under which the foundations of the "disease factories of the future" were laid. This background is furnished by various writers and in numerous reports: by Duncan himself, by his contemporary medical and other local co-operators such as Henry Smithers; in reports by Edwin Chadwick, Dr. Farr and others; in pamphlets from the Athenaeum Library, Liverpool (of which Duncan was a member from 1829 to 1863); and in references by Thomas Carlyle in *Chartists and Chartism* (the article entitled "The Finest Peasantry in the World"). Other interesting facts are included in Ramsay Muir's *History of Liverpool* and Hope's *Health at the Gateway*.

B

It is evident that Duncan was profoundly impressed by the housing conditions of Liverpool, but what impressed him even more was the extreme poverty associated with them. He therefore took every opportunity available to him to bring his views before the Town Council or magistrates either directly or through papers read before the Literary and Philosophical Society of Liverpool, some of the earlier of which date from 1842–3. In one of these papers he epitomized the situation by saying "the vicious construction of the dwellings, insufficient supply of out-offices and of receptacles for refuse and excrement, the absence of drains, deficient sewerage and overcrowding of the population is tending to increase the mortality of Liverpool." He commented especially upon the prevalence of typhus. Speaking specifically of cellars, in 1844 he said:

> The cellars are ten or twelve feet square; generally flagged—but frequently having only the bare earth for a floor, and sometimes less than six feet in height. There is frequently no window; so that light and air can gain access to the cellars only by the door, the top of which is often not higher than the level of the street. . . . There is sometimes a back cellar, used as a sleeping apartment, having no direct communication with the external atmosphere, and deriving its scanty supply of light and air solely from the first apartment.

The districts in which these evils were found at their worst were of course those to which the immigrants, mainly Irish, found their way. Duncan stated:

> It is they who inhabit the filthiest and worst ventilated courts and cellars, who congregate the most numerously in dirty lodging-houses, who are the least cleanly in their habits and the most apathetic about everything that befalls them.

It can scarcely be open to doubt that the evil sanitary

condition of the borough of Liverpool in the middle
years of last century was the direct cause of the high
mortality rate at all ages to which Duncan repeatedly
refers. To prove how high the mortality rate in Liverpool was at that time we can call to witness Dr. William
Farr, whose official title was that of Superintendent of
the Statistical Department of the Registrar-General's
Office, England. In 1885 the Sanitary Institute published a memorial volume containing a selection from
Farr's published work in connection with vital statistics
and it is from this compilation that the following
observations on mortality in Liverpool are extracted:

According to the life table, of 100,000 children
born in the healthy districts of England, 96,339 are
alive at the end of the first month, 3,661 having
died in the interval. Of the same number born in
Liverpool, only 94,551 are alive at the end of the
first month, 5,449 having died in the interval. At
the end of the second month 95,178 are alive in the
healthy districts, 1,161 having died in that month;
in Liverpool 92,088 are living, 2,463 having died in
the month; and so on until at the age of seven
months the numbers living are reduced to 91,932
in the healthy districts, and to 84,373 in Liverpool.

So unfavourable to infant life are the unsanitary
conditions of large towns—especially Liverpool—
that not only is the mortality at some months of age
twice as high as it is in the healthy districts, but at
seven months of age and upwards it is three times
as high. The mortality of infants by lung diseases
is higher in Liverpool than in any other large town.
The mortality of children under one year of age is
111 per 1,000 in the healthy districts of England, and
229 in Liverpool. . . .

Farr then gives a table (see Table I) showing the
number and proportion of deaths at different months
of age to 1,000 births in the healthy districts and in
Liverpool in the eight years 1839–46.

TABLE I

Months	Deaths		Proportion of deaths at each month of age to 1,000 *births*		Excess in Liver-pool
	In 63 Healthy Districts	In Liver-pool	In 63 Healthy Districts	In Liver-pool	
Total under 1 year	52,833	16,133	110·5	228·9	118·4
0 months	18,790	3,762	39·3	53.4	14·1
1 month	5,956	1,700	12·5	24·1	11·6
2 months	4,135	1,190	8·6	16·9	8·3
3 ,,	3,505	1,079	7·3	15·3	8·0
4 ,,	3,239	1,040	6·8	14·7	7·9
5 ,,	2,997	1,014	6·3	14·4	8·1
6 ,,	2,781	1,003	5·8	14·2	8·4
7 ,,	2,586	1,007	5·4	14·3	8·9
8 ,,	2,411	1,023	5·0	14·5	9·5
9 ,,	2,264	1,055	4·7	15·0	10·3
10 ,,	2,136	1,100	4·5	15·6	11·1
11 ,,	2,033	1,160	4·3	16·5	12·2

Note: The total births in the eight years 1839–46 were 478,048 in the Healthy Districts, and 70,491 in Liverpool.

Liverpool was, indeed, justifiably regarded at that time as the "Black Spot on the Mersey" and it is much to the credit of the authorities of the borough that in less than twenty years, by sanitary measures, they were able to reduce mortality rates to such an extent that Duncan could announce that in this respect Liverpool was superior to Manchester and other towns (see page 103). Farr might have been incredulous if someone had prophesied to him that a century later the infantile mortality rate in Liverpool as a whole was to be reduced to less than half that of his "healthy districts."

DR. WILLIAM FARR

The building of houses in *narrow* courts continued until the year 1842 when the Liverpool Building Act made this practice unlawful. The great majority of these houses were condemned and demolished towards the end of the nineteenth century and in the early years of the twentieth, especially during the time when Dr. E. W. Hope was Medical Officer of Health. The present writer has had the privilege of assisting at the obsequies of many of those that survived this ordeal.

Until the passing of the Municipal Corporations Act, 1835, the Borough of Liverpool was governed by a self-elected body. At that time the political complexion of the Council was Whig, but a few years later the Conservatives came into power. Whig or Tory the nineteenth-century Councils conformed to the traditions of the governing body of the borough in the eighteenth century. According to Ramsay Muir[1] the Council elected in 1835 was an "energetic, reforming Council which began vigorously to deal with police, sanitation, lighting and cleansing." During the next few years some slight progress was made with the construction of main sewers on the lines of a report by Mr. Rennie, the engineer, in 1815, who regarded the town as better adapted for a good system of sewering than any town in the Kingdom.

No estimate of cost was included in his recommendations and they do not appear to have been acted upon; while public opinion was divided as to the necessity of works of this kind, administrative authority was still more divided, being shared partly by magistrates, partly by the Council, partly by Commissioners and partly by the Poor Law authorities, for the work was thought to be too much for any one body to discharge.[2]

There is, however, no record of any marked progress in the direction of sewering the borough until after the Liverpool Sanitary Act of 1846.

[1] *History of Liverpool.*
[2] Professor E. W. Hope, *Health at the Gateway.*

2

EVENTS LEADING TO THE PASSING OF
THE LIVERPOOL SANITARY ACT, 1846

This Act—a private Act promoted by the Town Council—followed two important events. The first was a meeting convened by the Mayor in 1845 for the purpose of forming a Health of Towns Association, the main objects of which were "to bring the subject of sanitary reforms under the notice of every class of the community, to diffuse sound principles as widely as possible by meetings, lectures and publications, and especially to give information on all points connected with the sanitary condition of Liverpool and the means of improving it."[1] The second event was the publication by Dr. W. H. Duncan of a pamphlet entitled *The Physical Causes of the High rate of Mortality in Liverpool.* This pamphlet was based on two lectures which he had delivered in 1843 to the influential Liverpool Literary and Philosophical Society, of which he was treasurer for some years. A copy of this pamphlet is now in the library of the Public Health Department.[2]

Duncan, unlike Sir John Simon, wrote very little for publication. There is nothing from his pen corresponding to Simon's *English Sanitary Institutions.* We are, therefore, for the most part left to judge his character and abilities from his administrative work during the comparatively short time he was Medical Officer of Health of Liverpool, rather than from his writings.

[1] Professor E. W. Hope, *Health at the Gateway.*
[2] The contents of the pamphlet are practically identical with the summary of Duncan's evidence to the Commissioners for inquiring into the State of Large Towns and Populous Districts (First Report of the Commissioners, vol. i, p. 122), etc.

The only records available from which a judgment can be arrived at in regard to Duncan's attainments consist of a few pamphlets, a number of very short annual reports on the health of Liverpool from 1847 to 1862, transcripts of evidence given before committees of inquiry into sanitary conditions, and last, but not least, copies of letters written by him during the course of his official duties.

The most important of the very few pamphlets available is the one to which reference is made above. It was printed by Joshua Walmsley and, altogether, consists of seventy-six pages. As it seems to have been one of the factors which influenced the Town Council to take measures to promote the Liverpool Sanitary Act, 1846, it is well worth considering in some detail. In the pamphlet Duncan at once plunges *in medias res* by laying down the fundamental principle that "It has long been known that where a number of individuals are gathered together within a narrow compass, as in towns, the mortality among them considerably exceeds that occurring among an equal amount of population scattered over an extended surface, as in country districts." But the lecturer, already aware of the importance of statistics in connection with the public health and armed with the third annual report of the Registrar-General, does not expect his educated audience to take this statement on trust but immediately proceeds, by quoting carefully compiled figures, to prove it. His proof takes the form of a table in which he compares the mortality rates of "country districts," i.e. a number of counties grouped together, with low population densities, and the rates for "town districts" with high population densities. He has the wisdom to choose large figures. The total population for which death-rates are recorded is over 7,000,000 and the number of deaths is 396,000. Average densities of population in the "country districts" are 206 to the square mile and in the "town districts" 5,045, and mortalities are (as expressed by him) respectively 1 in 54·91 and

1 in 38·16. Further to impress upon his audience the difference in healthiness as between town and country Duncan mentions that the average age of death in two counties—Rutland and Wiltshire—was 36 years, and in four towns—Liverpool, Manchester, Leeds and Bolton—19 years. Here one feels that the future Medical Officer of Health of Liverpool was being more than a trifle tendentious in comparing counties with at least an average health record with four towns whose health records were atrociously bad.

Duncan then goes on to explain the causes of the difference between the mortalities of town and country districts in terms of the "miasmatic" theory of the transmission of communicable diseases. The one great cause, he says, which in its operation seems to absorb all others is the vitiation of the atmosphere of towns to effect which a number of agencies are constantly at work. By the mere action of the lungs of the inhabitants of Liverpool, for instance, a stratum of air sufficient to cover the entire surface of the town to the depth of three feet is *daily* rendered unfit for the purposes of respiration. To this main source of the vitiation of the atmosphere he adds the effects of the products of combustion from forges, furnaces and other fires, from gas, oil and candles nightly consumed in large quantities, and from the escape of gaseous effluvia from manufactories of different kinds.

Apart from this primary cause of ill-health (as he regarded it) in closely packed communities, he suggests that there were other factors. Wherever large masses of the community are gathered together a proportionately large amount of vegetable and animal refuse is produced which, in the process of decay, gives out various gases prejudicial to health; their dire effects will be increased by delay in the removal of the matter, or by its disposal in such a way as to allow the escape of the gases into the general atmosphere. From this point Duncan goes on to argue that this contamination of the atmosphere when people are closely crowded together is contagious and can affect the system with typhus and other fevers, and that this infection can spread with rapidity from individual to individual, from house to house, and from street to street. Duncan is, of course, aware of the value of efficient ventilation but he finds it difficult to attain in the working-class districts of large towns where, owing to the high value of land, houses have been constructed in courts and alleys around and within which the free circulation of air is impossible.

Duncan controverts the idea prevalent in lay circles that Liverpool is a healthy town.

About three years ago [he observes] I gave some evidence before the House of Commons Committee on the Health of Towns as to the prevalence of disease among the working classes and the high rate of mortality in Liverpool, which evidence (though a mere statement of fact) was stigmatized by some of the public authorities here (not, however, in their official capacity) as a foul and unmerited libel on the "good old town."

He then goes on to give his audience some figures in regard to the unhealthiness of Liverpool, compared with other large towns, saying that the causes of the high mortality in Liverpool, both absolutely and relatively, will be found to be the same as those of towns generally, but reach their maximum degree of intensity in Liverpool. Some of these causes he brings emphatically to the attention of his audience by discussing, with figures, the conditions under which by far the greater part of the population of the borough lived.

As some of the members present may not be acquainted with the character and construction of the courts in which so many of their townsmen reside I may state shortly that they consist usually of two rows of houses placed opposite to each other with an intervening space of from 9 to 15 feet, and having two to six or eight houses in each row. The court communicates with the street by a passage or archway about 3 feet wide—in the older courts built up overhead; and, the farther end being also in many instances closed by a high wall or by the back or side of an adjoining building, the court forms in fact a *cul-de-sac* with a narrow entrance. Such an arrangement almost bids defiance to the entrance of air, and renders its free circulation through the court a matter of impossibility.[1]

Duncan then describes the abominable insanitary conditions prevailing in the courts and cellars. Ashpits and privies were infrequently emptied and their contents consequently often spread over the court. "I do not know of a single court," he says, "which communicates with the street or sewer by a covered drain." In any case few of the streets in the working-class quarters of Liverpool in the year 1843 were sewered at all. According to Duncan's figures there were at that time $57\frac{1}{2}$ miles of streets in the parish of which $25\frac{1}{2}$ miles were either wholly or partially sewered. But sewering was being done unequally as between the various localities in the parish, the working-class districts where the density of population was greatest and the need most urgent being completed last.

In a later part of his paper Duncan expressed the opinion that another important element in the mortality was the unusual density of the population in Liverpool. Taking all the built-up areas, the number of persons per square mile in Liverpool was 138,224, while in Leeds it was 87,256. But some areas of Liverpool were much more densely populated than this. Duncan refers to Farr's report that in a small portion of London there were nearly 243,000 persons to the square mile; but says that in Liverpool there was a district containing about 12,000 inhabitants crowded

[1] At that time there were in the parish of Liverpool 1,982 courts, containing 10,692 houses, inhabited by 55,534 persons, i.e. more than one-third of the working-class population.

COURT WITH NARROW COVERED ENTRANCE

together on a surface of 105,000 square yards which gives a ratio of 460,000 inhabitants to the square mile. He goes still further and, confining his calculation to a portion of the same district with a population of 8,000 on 49,000 square yards, he obtains from this the proportion of 657,963 persons to the geographical square mile! This approaches the fantastic, but Duncan must have made a profound impression on his audience, if such figures had any meaning for them at all. Nevertheless, the point he was making was a perfectly sound one, as the overcrowding in the central areas of Liverpool in the middle of the last century was appalling. It may be well to mention here, although it is anticipating events a little, that even these figures of overcrowding, terrible as they are, do not quite plumb the depths of misery and degradation in which the casual labourers of Liverpool and their families had to live at that period. A few years later, in 1846 and 1847, Irish immigration added scores of thousands of people to the overcrowded courts and cellars of the borough and thereby increased the severity of the epidemics of cholera, typhus and other diseases which almost annually ravaged the working-class quarters.

Throughout the lectures Duncan repeatedly emphasized the evil effects of impure air which, in his view, besides carrying the causative agents of the fevers which were continually ravaging the populations of urban communities and prejudicing the general health, specially favoured the existence of "consumption" both in human beings and in animals, and "convulsions" in infants. He laid great stress on the sanitary conditions as the principal cause of Liverpool's high mortality:

A perusal of the evidence taken by the Select Committee on the Health of Towns will satisfy any one that in Liverpool and Manchester—which are the most unhealthy towns in the kingdom—the state of the dwellings of the working classes is also worse than in any other town in England; but that, in this respect, as well as in point of mortality, Liverpool is still lower in the scale than Manchester.

Prominent amongst the sanitary evils of the borough was the fact that a large percentage of the working-class population (one estimate gives 20 per cent.) lived in cellars, while many others lived in courts. Though an estimate of the number of persons living in courts is not given it was certainly much larger than the cellar population. Another source of mischief was found in the state of the dame schools and common day schools in the poorer parts of the city.

> In these schools where very little is even professed to be taught, and which are frequently held in cellars or in garrets, children are often crowded together, for two or three hours at a time, in numbers which soon render the atmosphere of these ill-ventilated apartments most oppressively close, and prejudicial to the health of the scholar—an effect which is evidenced by their exhausted looks and languid air after having been an hour or two confined.

One investigator, some years previously, had found that there were then in Liverpool 244 dame schools with 5,240 scholars and 194 common day schools with 6,096 scholars; that, with few exceptions, the dame schools were dark and confined and many damp and dirty; and that, in the case of the common day schools in the poorer districts, the atmosphere was so offensive in many of them as to be intolerable to a person entering from the open air.

Duncan ended his two lectures to the Literary and Philosophical Society by animadverting upon the sub-ordinate place which public health occupied in this country compared with the position in France and other Continental countries where the promotion of the public health was a constant object of solicitude both with the government and the municipal councils, and where important matters bearing on this point were only decided with the concurrence of the best professional and scientific opinion.

In 1844 Duncan published a further pamphlet in reply to criticisms by Mr. J. P. Halton, F.R.C.S., of statements in regard to the health of Liverpool made in the lectures to the Literary and Philosophical Society. Halton's pamphlet is not available but the nature of his criticisms can readily be inferred from Duncan's reply. It appears that Halton objected to the conclusions in regard to the general unhealthiness of Liverpool which Duncan drew from the tables published in his pamphlet and to the evidence given by Duncan before the House of Commons Committee on the Health of Towns. One statement in Halton's pamphlet was that Duncan's conclusion—"That judging from the annual proportion of deaths to the population, Liverpool is the most unhealthy town in England"—was at variance with the admission in another part of the pamphlet that there is a district in Liverpool (Rodney Street and Abercromby Wards) containing upwards of 30,000 inhabitants in which the mortality is below that of Birmingham—the most favoured in this respect of the large towns in England. If this was indeed a true summary of Halton's argument, it is not surprising that Duncan had little difficulty in disposing of it by pointing out the unfairness of using the mortality statistics of the most favoured residential districts in Liverpool as a sample of the whole borough. But Duncan's main refutation of the claims of Halton and others that Liverpool in 1843 was a healthy town (made presumably on patriotic rather than strictly factual grounds) was founded on the Registrar-General's figures which coldly stated that the yearly death-rate was $1:28\frac{3}{4}$ of the population compared with $1:36\frac{3}{4}$ in Birmingham and $1:37\frac{1}{2}$ in London.

This pamphlet was much discussed in the borough, and its results were considerable; indeed it seems to have been one of the factors which influenced the Town

Council—already the promoters of the useful Building Act of 1842—to further efforts in the cause of sanitary reform. But of course Liverpool was not alone in this forward movement. Sanitary reform was in the air at that time, largely owing to the efforts of that great public servant, Edwin Chadwick.

Chadwick, who was by profession a barrister, had early in life come under the influence of Jeremy Bentham (1748–1832) and he was one of a group of young men, which included Southwood Smith, Grote, Wakefield and James Mill, who all imbibed something of the spirit of the master. Primarily Bentham was a law reformer at a time when English Law with its harsh penal system and its emphasis on the rights of property urgently needed amendment; his proposals for the recasting of the legal system were based upon the utilitarian philosophy which had for its aim "the greatest happiness of the greatest number." This principle would be valueless unless practical steps of a political nature were taken in order to fulfil it, and in the hands of Bentham's disciples it led by gradual stages to penal reform, an extension of the suffrage, and an improvement in the sanitary conditions under which the poor (the greatest number) were then living in the rapidly growing industrial towns of this country. As Sir Henry Maine observed, "Bentham made the good of the community take precedence of every other object and thus gave escape to a current which had long been trying to find its way outwards."[1]

Chadwick became Bentham's secretary in 1830 and his legal knowledge was of great help when he was assisting the latter in the preparation of his Constitutional Code. This association with Bentham determined the future course of Chadwick's life. Instead of a lucrative practice at the Bar, for which his outstanding gifts well fitted him, Chadwick chose the hard and thorny path of a sanitary reformer and in 1832 accepted an appointment on Lord Grey's Poor Law Com-

[1] *Ancient Law.*

mission. From that day until the end of his career Chadwick's path was beset by opposition; he incurred the dislike of both the working classes and the propertied classes and in the end he was defeated and his personal career terminated. But he was to hand on the torch to others—to Southwood Smith and Sutherland of the General Board of Health, to Duncan of Liverpool and to John Simon of the City of London.

Under the Poor Law Amendment Act of 1834 Chadwick was appointed Secretary to the three Commissioners who were charged with the operation of the new scheme. He used this opportunity for an investigation into the causes of destitution. It came about in this way: in 1838 the Poor Law Commissioners wrote a letter to the Home Secretary (Lord John Russell) in which they mention that they had employed three medical inspectors to inquire into the prevalence and causation of preventable sickness and mortality in the Metropolis. In their view "The expenditure necessary to the adoption and maintenance of measures of prevention would ultimately amount to less than the cost of the disease now constantly engendered."[1] The salient point about this action of the Commission was that it had, for the first time, utilized the services of medical practitioners in connection with the inquiries which were being made, first in London and later in the provinces, into the health of the labouring population. Duncan was one of the numerous medical practitioners who submitted reports or evidence to the Poor Law Commission. His evidence, which is given in volume 2 of the Commission's Report, is dated 31st August, 1840, and is entitled *Report on the Sanitary State of the Labouring Classes in Liverpool*. He gives the population of the borough at that time as about 250,000, of which 175,000 belonged to the labouring classes. During the five years from 1835 to 1839, inclusive, there had been treated by the two dispensaries alone upwards of 25,000 cases of fever, giving a yearly average of 5,000.

[1] From Sir George Newman's *The Building of a Nation's Health*.

Counting in addition fever cases treated by club surgeons and private practitioners the total came to about 7,000 annually. Duncan then gives his reasons for these high totals.

There can be little doubt [he says] that the causes of the unusual prevalence of this disease in Liverpool are to be found principally in the condition of the dwellings of the labouring classes, who are almost exclusively its victims; but partly also in some circumstances connected with the habits of the poor.

With regard to their dwellings I would point out as the principal circumstances affecting the health of the poor:

1. Imperfect ventilation.

2. Want of places of deposit for vegetable and animal refuse.

3. Imperfect drainage and sewerage.

4. Imperfect system of scavenging and cleansing.

The circumstances derived from their *habits* most prejudicial to their health I conceive to be:

1. Their tendency to congregate in too large numbers under the same roof, etc.

2. Want of cleanliness.

3. Indisposition to be removed to the hospital when ill of fever.

Duncan further says: "Of the 175,000 individuals of the working classes, I estimate that nearly one-half inhabit courts. There are upwards of 8,000 inhabited cellars in Liverpool and I estimate their occupants at from 35,000 to 40,000." He refers to the need for places of deposit for animal and vegetable refuse and to an improvement in the sewerage system and says that the sewerage of Liverpool was so imperfect that, about two years previously, a local Act was procured appointing Commissioners with powers to levy a rate on the parish for the construction of sewers. This Act was due to expire the following year and under it £100,000 had been expended in the formation of sewers along the main streets, but many of these were still unsewered, and with regard to the streets inhabited by the working classes, he believed that the great majority were without sewers and that those which did exist were of a very imperfect kind. In his view there should be an authority to inspect and regulate lodging-houses, regulate the building of courts, and to prevent cellars being inhabited. Such an authority might well be formed by constituting Boards of Health in all large towns and getting them to employ Inspectors of Public Health.

Shortly before the time when Duncan read his paper before the Liverpool Literary and Philosophical Society the Poor Law Commission published its famous *Report on the Sanitary Condition of the Labouring Population of Great Britain.* This Report was presented to both Houses of Parliament in July, 1842, and led to the Royal Commission of 1843, appointed by Sir Robert Peel and presided over by the Duke of Buccleuch. This Commission fully confirmed Chadwick's findings and recommendations. Following the Report of the Royal Commission several sanitary Acts were passed, including the Public Health Act, 1848, for places outside London. Liverpool was, however, one step ahead of this legislation. Influenced by Duncan and others, and acting on the principle that desperate diseases require if not desperate at least urgent remedies, the Town Council promoted a private Bill in Parliament which became the Liverpool Sanitary Act, 1846.

C

3

SANITARY LEGISLATION IN
THE BOROUGH

It has already been said that Liverpool in the first half
of last century possessed a capable and energetic Town
Council which was sufficiently far in advance of its time
to realize the need for reform in the administration of
the borough, especially in regard to the improvement
of the environmental circumstances of the poorer-class
districts. The year in which the report of the Poor Law
Commission on the *Sanitary Conditions of the Labouring
Population of Great Britain* was laid before Parliament
saw the Town Council of the borough successful in
obtaining two private Acts—the Liverpool Improvement Act and the Liverpool Building Act. These are
not trivial pieces of legislation. The Improvement Act
contains 360 sections and the Building Act 131, and
they are most carefully drafted measures covering very
fully many aspects of the government of the borough.
The first-named Act deals generally with the good
government and police regulation of the borough but
also contains a number of sections dealing with the
handling of meat, the registration of existing slaughter-
houses and the licensing of new ones, the appointment
of inspectors, etc. But the Liverpool Building Act, as
it deals largely with sanitary measures, requires more
detailed notice.

As the long title states, it was an Act for the promotion of the Health of the Inhabitants of the Borough of
Liverpool and the better Regulation of Buildings in the
said Borough. One of the earlier sections of the Act
makes it mandatory on the Town Council to appoint
from among their number a committee to be called
"The Health Committee" for the purpose of exercising

the powers vested in the Council by the Act. The Act proceeds to deal with the appointment of surveyors to assist the Health Committee and it requires that at least one clear day's notice shall be given to the surveyor before any building should be begun to be erected or any addition or alteration made. Unlike modern Acts of Parliament which lay down general principles and leave the details to be dealt with in Regulations made by a Minister, the Liverpool Building Act, in section after section (sometimes varied by a reference to a Schedule) makes the most precise provision in regard to such matters as the thickness of party walls, the situation of flues and fireplaces, the heights of chimney shafts, the sizes of joists, purlins and rafters, the roofing of houses, and very many other matters of a similar kind. It is a very complete code governing the erection of new buildings, and it had the immediate effect of improving, to a marked extent, the standard of health and safety of the many dwellings which, at a time of rapid increase of population, were being erected in the borough.

It would be unrealistic to expect of our forefathers in 1842 the sanitary standards of the twentieth century; the Liverpool Building Act of 1842 had a number of defects, as was soon found when the surveyors, newly appointed by the Council, began to administer it, and it had to be radically amended four years later when a still more important piece of legislation—the Liverpool Sanitary Act, 1846[1]—was promoted by the Town Council.

The aims and objects of the Liverpool Sanitary Act, 1846, as they appeared to the officials of the Corporation who administered it, are well described by Mr. W. T. McGowen, the Principal Assistant to the Town Clerk, in a paper read to the Public Health Section of the National Association for the Promotion of Social Science in October, 1858:

---

[1] An Act for the Improvement of the Sewerage and Drainage of the Borough of Liverpool, and for making further Provisions for the Sanatory Regulation of the said Borough.

The principle of the Liverpool Act was purely that of Local Government. It entrusted enormous powers to the administrators, at the same time appointing for the office the Town Council, comprising gentlemen of high character and intelligence—a Government sufficiently permanent to induce the members to study the subject, popular enough to ensure a spirit of moderation, and familiar with local exigencies. The scope of the Act was so to deal with private rights as to make them subordinate to the public welfare. Thus, as the inhabiting of cellars unsuited for dwellings produced great mortality, their use was forbidden—as evil had resulted from houses being built without proper regard to light, ventilation or the decencies of life, regulations were established for enforcing attention to these requisites; summary power was given to justices to suppress nuisances certified by the Medical Officer as injurious to health; lodging houses were placed under control—narrow courts were prohibited. . . .

Two important doctrines were established: one that the owners of property, whose cupidity had done harm, and who would have to submit to sacrifices, got no compensation; another, that the new works should be executed at the cost of the partner to be benefited, namely, the Ratepayers, and not as was lately suggested for London and Galway, at the expense of others. . . .

The Corporation being clothed with authority for grappling with the existing mischief, soon found there was a difficult problem to solve. . . . The Health Committee on whom the task devolved, first selected as Engineer and Medical Officer, men of the highest talent they could find. . . .

It is bare justice to the public to say, that though "vested interests" have been often clipped during the past eleven years, the instances of resistance are trifling, whilst many persons have cheerfully yielded more than the Statute required.

This Act is indeed a monument to the sagacity and
foresight of the Liverpool Town Council of those days
and of the officials who advised them. With few precedents to guide them and in advance of the general Act
promoted by the Government—the Public Health Act,
1848[1]—the framers of the Liverpool Sanitary Act of
1846 succeeded in creating a sanitary code which established the Public Health Service as an essential activity
of local government. But the Liverpool Sanitary Act
did more than provide a sanitary code. It reduced to
something like order the chaotic system of authorities
which had up to that time administered such important
services as paving, sewering, drainage and cleansing in
the borough. In the Second Report of the Commission
of Inquiry into the *State of Large Towns and Populous
Districts* (1845) the peculiar complexity of the authorities dealing with those fundamental sanitary services
in Liverpool came in for strong criticism. Duncan had
given evidence to the Commission but the following
paragraphs are from the report of Dr. Lyon Playfair:

Before proceeding to an examination of the powers
granted by local Acts, I would refer to their want of
consolidation and inconvenient distribution to distinct and sometimes opposing authorities. For
example, the paving and sewerage of the streets of
Liverpool are entrusted to Commissioners, nine of
whom are members of the Corporation while fifteen
are independent of that body; the drainage and
paving of courts and alleys, on the other hand, are

[1] The most important administrative effect which followed the passing
of the Public Health Act, 1848, was the establishment—in the first
place for a period of five years—of the General Board of Health, a
central Department charged with the duty of supervising the work of
the local authorities. The life of the General Board was prolonged by
successive Acts of Parliament until 1858; but it had aroused so much
enmity throughout the country, largely because of its somewhat dic-
tatorial methods, that the pressure of public opinion finally forced its
discontinuance and its duties were in that year placed under the control
of the Privy Council.
One of the main weaknesses of the General Board of Health was that
it was not under the charge of a Minister and therefore its acts could
not be adequately explained and defended in Parliament.

severed from the authority exercising jurisdiction over the streets, and are entrusted to a committee of the Corporation appointed under the Act. Then the street cleansing is quite apart from either of these authorities, being placed under another and distinct committee of the Corporation and possessing no connection with the Commissioners of Sewers, although the legitimate object of the works executed by the latter is to preserve cleanliness in streets and in the houses adjoining; while, with strange incongruity, the "watering of streets" which is essentially connected with their proper cleansing, is removed from the scavenging authority and placed under that of the Commissioners of Sewers.

But this is not all; for the sewerage and cleansing of the borough is sub-divided, part of it (Toxteth Park) being governed by district Commissioners, quite independent of the authorities in the parochial part of Liverpool, as far, at least, as regards the paving and sewering of streets.

This chaos of conflicting and competing authorities was changed at a stroke by the Liverpool Sanitary Act of 1846 into a system which was at once simple and efficient. All the important functions referred to above —sewering, drainage, scavenging, paving and cleansing —were vested in the Town Council to be undertaken by a statutory committee of the Council—the Health Committee. Seldom has a recommendation of a Government Committee of Inquiry been brought into effect so quickly or with such beneficial consequences. In addition, apart from its administrative and sanitary provisions, this Act is noteworthy because it led to the appointment, for the first time, of the Medical Officer of Health, who, as an official, has played such a prominent part in local administration during the past hundred years. It is by no means certain who first suggested this title. According to Newman[1] the first specific proposal that "a district Medical Officer"

[1] Sir George Newman, *The Building of a Nation's Health.*

should be appointed locally, by the Crown or the local authority, was made in the general report on the *Sanitary Conditions of the Labouring Population of Great Britain* by Chadwick in 1842, in these words:

> That for the general promotion of the means necessary to prevent disease it would be good economy to appoint a district medical officer independent of private practice, and with the securities of special qualifications and responsibilities to initiate sanitary measures, and reclaim the execution of the law.

In the Liverpool Sanitary Act the idea sown by Chadwick in the Report comes to full development and the title of "Medical Officer of Health," so often repeated in sanitary and Public Health legislation during the next century, is used for the first time in an Act of Parliament. But the Act goes further than the mere creation of the title; it lays down in some detail the duties of the office:[1]

> And whereas the health of the population, especially of the poorer classes, is frequently injured by the prevalence of epidemical and other disorders, and the virulence and extent of such disorders, is frequently due and owing to the existence of local causes which are capable of removal but which have hitherto frequently escaped detection from the want of some experienced person to examine into and report upon them, it is expedient that power should be given to appoint a duly qualified medical practitioner for that purpose; Be it therefore enacted, that it shall be lawful for the said Council to appoint, subject to the approval of one of Her Majesty's Principal Secretaries of State, a legally qualified medical practitioner, of skill and experience, to inspect and report periodically on the sanitary condition of the said borough, to ascertain the existence of diseases, more especially epidemics increasing the rates of mortality, and to

[1] Liverpool Sanitary Act, 1846, Section 122.

point out the existence of any nuisances or other local causes which are likely to originate and maintain such diseases and injuriously affect the health of the inhabitants of the said borough, and to take cognisance of the fact of the existence of any contagious disease, and to point out the most efficacious modes for checking or preventing the spread of such diseases, and also to point out the most efficient means for the ventilation of churches, chapels, schools, registered lodging-houses, and other public edifices within the said borough, and to perform any other duties of a like nature which may be required of him; and such person shall be called the "Medical Officer of Health for the Borough of Liverpool"; and it shall be lawful for the said Council to pay such officer such salary as shall be approved of by one of Her Majesty's Principal Secretaries of State.

In order to deal more particularly with the sanitary condition of the borough, including the supervision of the scavengers and the abatement of nuisances, the Act reinforces the position of the Medical Officer of Health by requiring the Council to appoint an Inspector of Nuisances, who appears to be an officer independent of the Medical Officer of Health but obliged by the nature of his duties to work in close co-operation with him. The duties of the Inspector of Nuisances are laid down in Section 124 as follows:

And be it enacted, that it shall be lawful for the said Council, and they are hereby required to nominate and appoint one or more persons to superintend and enforce the due execution of all duties to be performed by the scavengers appointed under this Act, and to report to the said Council and Health Committee all breaches of the bye-laws, rules and regulations of the said Council and Health Committee, and to point out the existence of any nuisances, and such person shall be called "The Inspector of Nuisances," and the said Council and Health Committee shall require such Inspector to provide and keep a

book, in which shall be entered all complaints made
by any inhabitant of the said borough of any infringe-
ment of the provisions of this Act, or of the bye-
laws, rules and regulations made by the said Council
for the preservation of due order as may be required
by the said Council and Health Committee: and such
Inspector shall forthwith inquire into the truth or
otherwise of such complaints, and report upon the
same to the said Health Committee at their next
meeting, and such report, and the order of the said
Health Committee thereon, shall be entered in the
said book, which shall be kept at the office of the
said Town Clerk, and shall be open at all reasonable
times to the inspection of any inhabitant within the
said borough; and it shall be the duty of such
Inspector, subject to the direction of the said Council
and Health Committee, to make complaints before
any Justice, and take legal proceedings for the
punishment of any person or persons for any offence
under this Act, or under any bye-laws made by
virtue thereof.

The two officials—the Medical Officer of Health and
the Inspector of Nuisances—are separated in the Act
by a single section, but officially (in the case of the
Inspector of Nuisances, for part of the time, under a
different name) they have been inseparable for a century
and their partnership has produced highly beneficial
results in the sphere of public health.

Some other sections of this important Act deserve
mention. In general it is enacted that the Mayor,
Aldermen and Burgesses of the Borough of Liverpool
are, through the Council, entrusted with the duty of
executing the Act and its powers; but, as in the case
of the Liverpool Building Act, 1842, certain functions
are delegated to the Health Committee. The Act makes
the Council the surveyors of highways; the control of
the streets is vested in them, and the Council is given
power to cause the streets to be paved. One section
forbids the erection of any more narrow courts of the

type nine to fifteen feet wide, which had proved such a serious sanitary evil in Liverpool for many years. The section referred to continues to permit the erection of courts but they had to be of a clear width of fifteen feet and, if containing more than eight houses, an additional foot was to be added to the width of the court for each additional house. Each entrance passage had to be of the same width as the court and building over the entrance was prohibited, as also were buildings of a height greater than 30 feet or of more than two stories above ground. One important section (61) places an obligation upon the Council, with all convenient dispatch, to sewer and drain the borough. All sewers, from the date of the Act coming into operation, are vested in the Mayor, Aldermen and Burgesses and pass under the control of the Council. It was under these provisions that the great undertaking of sewering the borough between the years 1847 and 1868 was carried through.

Some of the remaining provisions may be briefly noted. It was forbidden to erect a house without drains; vaults and cellars were not to be made without the consent of the Council; gulleys were to be fitted with traps; power was given to enforce the abatement of nuisances injurious to health; there were regulations to prevent the accumulation of dung and powers to prevent the forming of pools of stagnant water; no house in future was to be built without a privy and, if necessary, an ashpit, and owners had to keep these in repair; and it became lawful for the Council to provide public conveniences. One provision of interest is that, under Section 120, it was enacted that no house should thereafter be erected in the borough without at least one room on the ground floor containing 108 superficial feet of area. A further provision laid it down that in every room in a house used for habitation there had to be one external window five feet at least in height and three feet wide, clear of the sash-frame, and it was made unlawful to let separately for habitation any cellar under any house in a court.

SMALL COURT WITH HIGH BUILDINGS AT END

The above description is intended only to give some idea of the scope of the Act of 1846. Promoted by a local authority and not by the Government it exercised a profound effect upon the general sanitary legislation of the country for many years. It influenced the drafting of the Public Health Act of 1848, and the example set by it in regard to the appointment of a Medical Officer of Health was followed in the next year by the City of London, and in subsequent years by many other local authorities. The Liverpool Sanitary Act was essentially a practical measure: it not only laid down a code of sanitary rules but it provided the administrative machinery to enforce these rules—the Town Council as a highway authority, the Health Committee as the agent of the Council to execute the provisions of the Act, and appropriate officials such as the Medical Officer of Health, the Surveyor and the Inspector of Nuisances, charged with the duty of carrying out the decisions of the statutory authorities.

In practice some portions of the Act proved difficult to administer and a number of amendments were introduced by the Liverpool Sanitary Amendment Act, 1854. The Liverpool Sanitary Act (usually referred to by officials in their reports as the "Sanatory[1] Act") came into operation on the 1st January, 1847, and immediate action was taken by the Town Council to bring into force some of its provisions. Preliminary arrangements to make certain appointments had, indeed, been agreed to by the Council late in the year 1846, in anticipation of the statute, as, for example, the issue of an advertisement, dated 11th December, for a "qualified Civil Engineer to act as Local Surveyor." As a result of this advertisement Mr. James Newlands was appointed to that post on the 26th January, 1847. He, like the Medical Officer of Health and the Inspector of Nuisances, was to work under the Health Committee of the Town

---

[1] The spelling of the word has undergone a change. In Duncan's day it was "Sanatory." I have used the modern spelling except in quotations. There is no short title to the Act of 1846, so that I feel it permissible to use the modern spelling when referring to it.

Council which was already in being, having been
appointed under the provision of Section 2 of the
Liverpool Building Act, 1842.

So the stage was set for the gigantic work of improving the sanitary condition of the borough of
Liverpool, and even in the few years immediately following the passing of the Act great progress was made
in sewering, draining and paving the streets and houses
of the town and in supervising cellars, courts and
lodging-houses. In 1850 the Health Committee instructed the Borough Engineer, the Medical Officer of
Health and the Inspector of Nuisances to submit progress reports covering the work done by the three
departments during the four years 1847–50 inclusive.
These reports were printed and bound together in a
single volume, a copy of which is in the present Public
Health Department's library. This volume affords a
clear indication of the immense volume of work which
those officers performed in the period of four years
towards the sanitary improvement of the borough.
Such rapid progress in such a short period of time
could never have been effected if the departmental
officers had not been fully supported by a Health Committee and a Town Council willing to make prompt
decisions and to incur the very heavy expenditure
involved in carrying them out. But by that time the
need for sanitary reform in all the large towns in this
country had been abundantly proved as a result of the
work of Chadwick, Farr, Duncan and Simon, and, in
an age which was no stranger to reforms in the political
and social spheres, action seldom lagged long behind
the demonstrated need for it. That the borough of
Liverpool became a leader and pioneer in the sphere
of sanitation was partly due to the civic pride and local
patriotism of the Town Council and partly to the overwhelming need for an improvement in the circumstances under which such a large proportion of their
population lived in the courts and cellars of the industrial quarters of the town.

4

APPOINTMENT OF DUNCAN AS
MEDICAL OFFICER OF HEALTH

THE choice of the Town Council for the newly created
post of Medical Officer of Health was not a matter of
doubt, and on the 1st January, 1847, the appointment
of William Henry Duncan to that office was confirmed
by the Secretary of State as required by the Liverpool
Sanitary Act of 1846. His salary on appointment was
£300 per annum with the right to private practice[1]

[1] *Punch*, in one of its early issues published in the year 1847 (Vol.
XII, p. 44), had some critical comments to make about the salary to be
paid by the Liverpool Corporation for this part-time appointment.

"By the papers *Mr. Punch* learns that the Town Council of Liverpool
intend to appoint an Officer of Health, whose duties will consist in the
direction of their sanatory arrangements, and whose services they pro-
pose to remunerate by a salary of £300 a year, with the liberty to
augment that handsome income, if he can, by private practice.

"*Mr. Punch* will engage to find a competent person, who will willingly
undertake the responsibilities of this office, on the liberal terms proposed
by the Town Council of Liverpool.

"*Mr. Punch*, on behalf of the respectable medical gentleman, his
nominee, will promise that he, the said respectable medical gentleman,
shall devote his full attention to his official duties, and endeavour to
make money by private practice only at those few leisure moments
when he shall have nothing else to do. For, although a practitioner of
any eminence expects, generally, to make at least a thousand a year,
this gentleman shall regard his situation, bringing him in £300, as of
primary importance, and shall look upon his private earning as matters
of secondary considerations.

"If the Officer of Health recommended by *Mr. Punch* shall have for a
patient a rich butcher, with a slaughter house in a populous neighbourhood; an opulent fellmonger or tallow-chandler, with a yard or manufactory in the heart of town, he shall not hesitate from motives of
interest to denounce their respective establishments as nuisances. He
shall not fail to point out the insalubrity of any gas-works, similarly
situated, the family of whose proprietor he may attend; and if any
wealthy old lady who may be in the habit of consulting him shall infringe
the Drainage Act, he shall not fail to declare the circumstances to the
authorities.

but this was soon found to be incompatible with his public duties and the terms of his appointment were soon altered to full-time service, with an annual salary of £750. The resolution of the Council appointing Duncan as *full-time* Medical Officer of Health of the borough was as follows:

Council, 11th January, 1848.

Resolved unanimously—That William Henry Duncan, Doctor of Medicine, be, and he is hereby (subject to the approval of one of Her Majesty's Principal Secretaries of State and to the provisions of the local act of the session of 1846, intituled "An Act for the Improvement of the Sewerage and Drainage of the Borough of Liverpool, and for making further provisions for the sanitary regulation of the said Borough") appointed during the pleasure of the Council, the Medical Officer of Health for the Borough of Liverpool, at a salary of £750 per annum, it being understood that he is to give up all private practice and to devote the whole of his time and attention to the duties of the said office.[1]

Some years later Duncan refers to the terms and conditions of his appointment in a letter to a correspondent (25th February, 1854) who evidently had some proper interest in the matter:

In compliance with the request of Mr. —— communicated to me by the Rev. Mr. —— I have much pleasure in forwarding to you the accompanying statement of my duties as Medical Officer of Health for the Borough of Liverpool.

The salary attached to the office is £750. An office with the necessary expenses of stationery, etc. is provided by the Corporation and in times of unusual

---

"*Mr. Punch* repeats, that he will pledge himself to produce an able and experienced medical practitioner, who shall fulfil all these conditions; but he respectfully asks the Town Council of Liverpool who, but himself, would for a moment encourage them to expect such a man—for their money."

[1] Paid Officers' Committee Rept., 1851.

pressure of business, the salary of a clerk is also allowed. The duties here are quite incompatible with private practice. In the first instance the salary was fixed at £300 per annum, but the arrangement was found so inconvenient that at the recommendation of the Secretary of State (whose sanction is required to the salary as well as the appointment) the salary was increased to its present amount, my whole time being required to be devoted to my public duties.

I accepted the salary on the understanding that it would be increased after a time.

I agree with the Secretary of State and the Sanitary Commissioners in thinking that the duties cannot be faithfully performed (at least in such a town as Liverpool) by a medical man in practice without incurring the risk of injuring his private interests.

Although Duncan's appointment was stated in the Town Council's resolution to be "during the pleasure of the Council," as were the appointments of most of the other senior officials, it seems as if within a short period of time some representations must have been made to the Secretary of State with the object of affording the holder of the post of Medical Officer of Health some security of tenure, because at the end of his first progress report to the Health Committee—covering the years 1847 to 1850—Duncan makes the following observations:

> In conclusion the experience of the last three years has shown the wisdom of the Sanitary Commissioners and of the Secretary of State in recommending that the appointment which I have the honour to hold should be placed on an independent footing; for the duties, if faithfully discharged, are of such a nature as inevitably to bring the Officer of Health into collision with those whose private interests they may affect, and some of whom might feel disposed to exercise any power they possessed to injure him in his professional capacity.

Most Medical Officers of Health will to-day be in agreement with this opinion so cogently expressed by the first holder of their office. Nor has the lapse of time rendered this opinion less valid. The very nature of the duties of a Medical Officer of Health, especially in connection with sanitation and housing, renders him peculiarly liable to incur personal animosities from which he should receive all possible protection. This measure of protection which is to-day afforded by law to the majority of Medical Officers of Health enables them to do their duty without fear or favour, and is of undoubted benefit to the communities they serve.

Duncan was forty-two years of age at the time of his appointment. Besides being Physician to the South Dispensary (then situated at 1 Upper Parliament Street) he was lecturer in Medical Jurisprudence in the Medical School at the Royal Institution. In the session 1844–5 he gave a course of lectures on Materia Medica and Therapeutics. At the same time he was one of the physicians to the Royal Infirmary (then situated in Shaw's Brow) and lived at 18 Rodney Street. He had taken a prominent part in the professional and social life of the borough and besides being a member of the Athenaeum (then in the Church Street building) was also a member of the Liverpool Medical Institution. In 1837 he was appointed one of the four yearly Presidents of the Liverpool Medical Society. It is on record that he subscribed a sum of £5 towards the erection of the present Medical Institution building and that he was one of the subscribers to Baines's *History of Liverpool* published in 1852.

Hitherto he had come into contact with the poor of Liverpool as an individual medical practitioner. It remained to be seen whether his skill as a doctor dealing with individual patients could be successfully turned into the field of administration. Without any precedents to guide him, without resources of any kind, he had to organize a Public Health Department from the beginning, to lay down rules of administration and procedure, to train such staff as might from time to time be allotted to him, and to fit himself and his activities into the framework of the Town Council's organization. His knowledge of the principles governing the transmission of communicable diseases was no greater than that of the medical profession of his time, and although his experience as Physician to the South Dispensary had well qualified him to recognize the principal zymotic diseases and to treat them after the accepted manner, it did not materially assist him to perform what was his statutory duty—namely to ascertain the causes of such diseases and to point out the most efficacious modes of checking or preventing their spread. Duncan had had much experience of cholera, especially in the 1832 epidemic in Liverpool, and he was one of the medical practitioners who were specially thanked by the Board of Health for services during that year.[1]

Duncan's paper read to the Literary and Philosophical Society showed that he had fairly clearly defined ideas as to the origins of communicable diseases. They were, in his view, caused by poisonous emanations into the atmosphere derived from the human body during the process of respiration. These emanations only became dangerous when the atmosphere within a confined space was foul as a result of a lack of ventilation. Such a theory was not readily adapted to explain specificity of infection, or, at least, Duncan never in his writings discusses this point. But even when convinced that the atmospheric or miasmatic theory of the transmission of infectious diseases was the true one he seemed at times to doubt whether this supposition explained all the facts known to him. As we shall see later he was in some difficulty with the theory when he came to face the facts of the 1849 cholera outbreak during which (as he realized) many persons were directly infected from the secretions and from handling the bodies of persons dying from the disease.

[1] T. H. Bickerton, H. R. Bickerton and R. M. B. MacKenna, *Medical History of Liverpool.*

D

The broad lines of the duties attached to the new post of Medical Officer of Health had been laid down in Section 122 of the Liverpool Sanitary Act, but it became necessary when Duncan commenced work in January, 1847, to define for himself the precise manner in which he should develop the administrative side of his appointment. It was as clear to him as to those who appointed him that his principal duty was to devise some method of controlling the epidemics of infectious diseases—of which the most dreaded was cholera—which year by year ravaged the poorer quarters of the borough, occasionally overflowing into more opulent districts such as Rodney Street and Abercromby Square. If the Medical Officer of Health could reduce the impact of the major infectious diseases upon the crowded populations of the cellars and courts of industrial Liverpool by any methods which he could devise, his appointment to the newly created office would be abundantly justified. If he failed to attain this end, the borough would be helpless and unprotected until the day came when medical science would discover the precise causation of these diseases and thus point the way to methods of prevention. Duncan's vague theories of the origins of communicable diseases, imperfect as they were, possessed the great advantage that they led to the right solution of the vast problem of reducing the incidence of cholera, typhoid and dysentery in the industrial towns of England during the nineteenth century. The right solution at that stage of our social history was efficient sanitation—the cleansing of the streets and houses of the thickly populated towns by the removal of organic matter from their neighbourhood. This solution was not new; it had been advocated by all the commissions which year by year had been reporting on the health of towns. But to improve the sanitation of the large industrial towns meant the expenditure of large sums of money on engineering works of various kinds and a number of years were to go by before the sewering and drainage and cleansing of the borough of Liverpool had become so efficient that serious epidemics of infectious diseases of intestinal origin ceased to be a main preoccupation of the Town Council and the Boards of Guardians.

No correspondence of Duncan's is available for the years 1847 and 1848 and his first progress report was not written until 1851. It is not, therefore, possible to discover what were his immediate reactions to the manifold problems of his new appointment. His more mature views on his duties and responsibilities are disclosed in a letter dated the 9th November, 1853, as follows:

Absence from home and the pressure of other engagements have prevented an earlier reply to your letter of the 24th October.

The only definition of the duties of Medical Officer of Health in this borough is contained in the 122nd, 123rd and 133rd clauses of 9 and 10 Vict. C. 127 (our local Sanatory Act). The 122nd clause states that he is "to inspect and report periodically on the sanitary condition of the borough, to ascertain the existence of diseases, more especially epidemics increasing the rates of mortality, and to point out the existence of any nuisances or other local causes which are likely to originate and maintain such diseases, and injuriously affect health, etc. and to point out the most efficacious modes for checking or preventing the spread of such diseases, and also to point out the most efficient means for the ventilation of churches, chapels, schools, registered lodging-houses and other public edifices, etc. and to perform any other duties of a like nature.

The 123rd clause empowers the Health Committee to compel owners to whitewash, cleanse or purify houses certified by the Officer of Health to be in a filthy or unwholesome condition, and the 133rd clause states that if any Candle House, Melting House, Soap House, Boiling House, Bone Store, or any manufactory be certified by the Officer of Health as a nuisance and injurious to health, the Health Committee may take proceedings to abate the nuisance.

An important part of my duties, not specified as such in the Act but referred to in the 125th clause and also in the Bye-laws relates to the Lodging-houses, all of which have to be inspected previous to registration, with a view to fixing the number of lodgers to be allowed in each, and which, did my other duties permit, ought also to be periodically inspected afterwards. Nearly 2,000 of these houses have been already inspected.

The Bye-laws regarding slaughter-houses will inform you of my duties in connection with them.

I make weekly, quarterly and annual reports of the health of the town, founded on the Register of Deaths, copies of which are forwarded weekly by the different Registrars, and which are analysed and digested on the system adopted by the Registrar-General.

The localities indicated by these registers or by other sources of information as the seat of zymotic disease, are visited with the view of ascertaining the existence of local and removable causes, giving advice to the survivors, and taking the necessary measures as regards drainage, cleansing, etc. Any streets which require sewerage or paving, etc. on sanitary grounds, are reported to the Committee at their weekly meetings, and I also report on any special subject which may be referred to me.

The visiting of the ill-conditioned localities with a view of detecting the existence of removable causes of disease will probably form, at the present time, the most important part of your duties as Sanitary Inspector. You will also, I presume, be called on to advise as to the measures necessary to be adopted in anticipation of the approach of cholera.

I enclose copies of our Lodging-house and

Slaughter-house Bye-laws, also forms for the measurement of lodging-houses and of application to register, and of the forms used for proceedings under the Nuisances Removal Act.

In January, 1847, Duncan began the task of forming a new department, and in this he received advice and assistance from his colleagues, the chief officers of the other Corporation's services. Unstinted help from one department to another is the rule to-day in the Local Government Service and there is no reason to suppose that the new Medical Officer of Health applied in vain to the Town Clerk, Treasurer or Head Constable of the Liverpool of those days for such advice or help as these long-established colleagues were able to give. There is a good deal of information about the officers of the Corporation at that time and much of it is collected in convenient form in the report, dated 1851, of a Special Committee of the Town Council appointed for the purpose of inquiring into the respective duties of all the paid officers of the Corporation, and the amounts of salary attaching to them, with a view to such reduction of the number of officials or their salaries as might be consistent with the efficient working of the Corporation. This early prototype of the Geddes Axe does not appear to have accomplished much in the way of reduction of staff or salaries, but the report is interesting because it gives the names, salaries and duties of all—or practically all—the officers employed by the Council, including the office-boy in the Town Clerk's Department, who was sixteen years of age, resided in William Henry Street, was in receipt of 6s. per week and of whom it is said, "He is now becoming pretty useful."

The Town Clerk was Mr. William Shuttleworth, who at that time was forty-three years of age and resided at 113 Mount Pleasant. He was appointed by the Council on the 9th November, 1844, on the death of Mr. Richard Radcliffe. The salary attaching to the

office of Town Clerk was (for those days) the generous
one of £2,000 per annum. It is said in the report that
office hours were from 9 a.m. to 5 p.m. for the whole
of the establishment of this department but that it was
necessary for the Town Clerk and the Head Clerks in
the different departments to take home papers or
documents.

The office of Treasurer was really a dual one, consisting of the Borough Treasurer and the Health
Treasurer. The Borough Treasurer was Mr. John
Wybergh and the Treasurer to the Health Committee
Mr. Capes Ashlin, the salaries attaching to these offices
being respectively, in 1851, £700 and £600 per
annum. In regard to these two offices the Committee
make the wise suggestion that, on a vacancy occurring,
the posts should be amalgamated at a salary of £750
per annum.

The Surveyor, Mr. John Weightman, was at this
time fifty-two years of age and had been appointed in
1848 at a salary of £1,000 per annum. His duties consisted of the general superintendence and management,
under the Finance Committee, of the estate and property of the Corporation, which was then, and still is, a
very large undertaking.

Probably the most famous of Duncan's colleagues
was the Borough Engineer. Mr. James Newlands was
then thirty-six years of age. He was appointed by the
Council on the 26th January, 1847, and his appointment
was confirmed by the Secretary of State in February,
1847. In the advertisement issued for this post it was
stated that the person appointed was to be a qualified
Civil Engineer and that his duties were to act as Local
Surveyor of the Sewerage, Drainage, Paving and other
works authorized by the Liverpool Sanitary Act, 1846.
The salary was £700 per annum.

Of all officers in charge of separate departments the
one most closely in touch with the Medical Officer of
Health was the Inspector of Nuisances. He was at this
time Mr. Thomas Fresh, aged forty-seven, and living at

1 St. Mary's Lane, Hope Street. He was appointed on the 4th January 1847. His hours of duty were from 8 a.m. to 6 p.m. and his salary was £170 per annum.

Besides the Inspector there were employed at that time in this department a chief clerk, two midden clerks, a report clerk and a notice and cellar clerk, an outdoor staff, consisting of two Assistant Inspectors, four cellar officers and a supplementary staff composed of two officers whose duties were to keep a check upon the general sanitary condition of the town and to take the dimensions of lodging-houses for the Medical Officer of Health.

A number of registers were kept in this office, including those dealing with cellars, smoke nuisances, lodging-houses and knackers' yards; and books were used in which were entered particulars of middens, nuisances, cellars, lodging-houses, slaughter-houses, etc., including any action taken in regard to them. One of the several "nuisance" books contained complaints made by the Medical Officer of Health. This book passed daily between the Medical Officer of Health and the Inspector of Nuisances.

5

TWO CALAMITOUS YEARS

DUNCAN's progress report covering the years 1847–50 is short and deals almost entirely with the epidemic situation in the borough. In this account of the health of the borough written in 1851, he says that of the four years which had elapsed since the Liverpool Sanitary Act of 1846 came into operation, "Two of these years are memorable as seasons of the severest epidemic visitations from which Liverpool has suffered within the period of authentic records; and with regard to these it has been thought proper to enter somewhat into detail, as a document for future reference."

Duncan had entered upon his duties at a very critical time, from the epidemiological point of view, in the history of the borough. The preceding year (1846) had been one of unusually high mortality caused by the prevalence of epidemic dysentery during the summer months, followed by fever; but at the close of the year the mortality of the town was rapidly subsiding to its ordinary standard.

At the beginning of his first year's report—for 1847 —Duncan, in some alarm, refers to the fact that Irish paupers, driven from their miserable cabins by fear of starvation, were landing in Liverpool in large numbers.[1]

[1] This flight of the poorer people was occasioned by the Irish potato famine which commenced in 1845 and reached disastrous proportions in 1846 and 1847, causing widespread starvation. The failure of the crop was due to the potato blight, a small fungus known scientifically as *Phytophthora infestans*. The potato was at that time the staple food of the Irish people as it normally grows well under a heavy rainfall and in peaty soils. Unfortunately famine relief arrangements were only slowly brought into force and were unimaginatively administered, with the result that many people starved to death while others, more able or more adventurous, crowded into the ships leaving for England.

The 1st of January, 1847 [he says], found this pauper immigration steadily increasing, and it continued in such rapidly progressive rates, that by the end of June not less than 300,000 Irish had landed in Liverpool. Of these it was very moderately estimated that from 60,000 to 80,000 had located themselves amongst us, occupying every nook and cranny of the already overcrowded lodging-houses, and forcing their way into the cellars (about 3,000 in number) which had been closed under the provisions of the Health Act, 1842. In different parts of Liverpool 50 or 60 of these destitute people were found in a house containing three or four small rooms, about 12 feet by 10; and in more than one instance upwards of 40 were found sleeping in a cellar.

The report indicates that some anxiety was being felt in Governmental circles about this influx of refugees into an already overcrowded town, and in February of that year Duncan was asked to draw up a report for the information of the Secretary of State. Fever had already become more than usually prevalent, especially in the lodging-houses hopelessly overcrowded by the immigrants, and Duncan was facing what he recognized as being a critical situation with no medical staff, no hospitals except Poor Law Institutions, and the virtual certainty of a severe epidemic. So he reported "should the destitute Irish continue to flock into Liverpool as they are still doing, there can be little doubt that what we now see is only the commencement of the most severe and desolating epidemic which has visited Liverpool for the last ten years." This prophecy did not long await fulfilment. By the middle of the year the mortality from fever had risen to 2,000 per cent. above the average of former years. Later on in the year 1847 there were at one time between 4,000 and 5,000 cases (exclusive of those in hospital) under the care of the dispensary and parish medical officers—this in a population in the parish of less than 250,000. Attempts

were made to provide some accommodation for the
cases, and hospital after hospital was opened in different
districts of the town; the lazarettoes in the river were,
by consent of the Government, converted into hospital
ships, and still the cases admitted to hospital were
more than twice outnumbered by those for which no
hospital accommodation was provided. In the beginning
of May the epidemic burst through the barriers which
had hitherto seemed to confine it to the poorer classes
of the inhabitants; it invaded the better-conditioned
districts of the town, establishing itself among the
English population, who had previously escaped its
ravages, and gradually creeping up among the wealthier
classes of society.

Early in the autumn the tide of Irish immigration
had begun to slacken, and in November I reported
to the Committee that the inferior lodging-houses
were not more crowded than usual in ordinary times.

Duncan gives a number of tables showing the mortalities in the various wards from "Fever" and "Diarrhoea." "Fever" (sometimes called Irish Famine Fever)
was undoubtedly mainly typhus and typhoid, and "Diarrhoea" included many cases of dysentery. Altogether in
the borough during the year 1847 5,845 persons died
from fever and 2,589 from diarrhoea.[1] He also gives
examples of the total deaths in various wards. Thus in
the Vauxhall Ward nearly one-seventh of the population
was swept away in the course of the year, while in the
wealthy Rodney Street and Abercromby Wards the
total mortality was less than one in twenty-eight. The
latter and much more favourable figure, involving a
death-rate of 35, would appear sufficiently alarming to a
modern sanitarian accustomed to death-rates for a
whole city of less than 12, but the figure for the Vauxhall Ward—a death-rate of 135—would seem cata-
strophic. In Lace Street one-third of the ordinary popu-

[1] These totals included ten medical practitioners and ten Roman
Catholic priests.

lation of several hundred persons died in the course of the year. As for the Parish of Liverpool as a whole, more than one-fourteenth perished during the year. Duncan estimates that in 1847 nearly 60,000 persons in the borough suffered from fever and nearly 40,000 from diarrhoea and dysentery. It was the most fatal year in the history of Liverpool.

Duncan's report for the year 1848 begins on a much more optimistic note. There were indeed three epidemics in progress—scarlatina in its early stage, influenza in its middle period, and the Irish fever—as he calls it—in its decline. As regards the last-named the deaths, which were 60 in the borough in the first week of January, declined to 24 by the last week of March, and to 11 by the end of May, when the epidemics might be considered as having been extinguished after an existence of seventeen months. The epidemic of scarlatina, however, continued and by the end of the year had caused 1,516 deaths amongst a population of little more than a third of that of present-day Liverpool—the main incidence, as always, appearing amongst the overcrowded dwellings of the poor, and passing by, or only slightly affecting, the habitations of the wealthy. The Medical Officer of Health does note as a point of interest that this epidemic of scarlatina seems to be in a less degree than typhus under the influence of an impure atmosphere. He is by no means as certain now as he was several years previously in his lectures to the Literary and Philosophical Society that infectious diseases generally are the results of non-specific atmospheric contamination. But he does argue that scarlatina spreads more rapidly and, as a general rule, assumes a more aggravated form in the comparatively filthy and crowded districts. Typhus, he thinks, appears seldom in clean and airy localities, scarlatina more frequently.

During the year 1848, within the borough, there were 4,350 deaths from zymotic diseases and 1,400 from consumption.

The year 1849 was noteworthy as the year of epidemic cholera. Duncan traces the origin of this pandemic from India—its birthplace—in 1846, through Persia and Russia in the following year, traversing the north of Europe, by Berlin and Hamburg, and reaching Edinburgh on the 1st October, 1848. In November it became epidemic in Glasgow and Dumfries, in both places raging with great severity. On the 10th December an Irish family arrived in Liverpool by steamer from Dumfries, where the epidemic was then at its height. On landing, one of the children was found to be suffering from cholera and both parents went down with the disease on the night of their arrival in Liverpool. All these cases proved fatal and on the 15th a woman residing in the same house, who had washed the bodies of the deceased and also bedclothes, etc., was attacked by the disease and died after twelve hours' illness. The first undoubted case of Liverpool origin occurred on the 16th in a crowded house in a court in Back Portland Street, the victim being a girl about fourteen years of age. Next day her father and a younger sister were attacked and all three died. Some action appears to have been taken by Duncan's Department at this stage, as the remaining inmates of the house were removed and the houses in the court were limewashed. No doubt the removal of actual or potential sources of infection was effective and for a time the disease spread no further in that locality. Such cases as had occurred so far were undoubtedly case to case infections or infections through the medium of fomites, and the removal of infected persons, bedding and contacts would be sufficient to impose a local check on the epidemic. Unfortunately, however, on the 18th a woman residing in a comparatively clean and airy apartment in Fylde Street, Toxteth Park, about $2\frac{1}{2}$ miles away from Back Portland Street, took ill with cholera and died. No contacts between the case and the previous cases could be traced. As far as Duncan was aware no further case of Asiatic cholera occurred within the borough until the 15th January, 1849, although he admits that a case which came to his notice late in December, 1848, and which was registered as a death from "diarrhoea," did occur. Early in 1849 there was no undue prevalence of diarrhoea and the health of the town appeared satisfactory. However, on the 15th January a case of cholera occurred and several more were reported before the end of the month. In addition a small number of cases were imported from Glasgow.

TABLE II

Week ending		Cholera Deaths	Week ending		Cholera Deaths
May	5	11	August	4	368
,,	12	18	,,	11	412
,,	19	20	,,	18	572
,,	26	25	,,	25	406
June	2	41	September	1	383
,,	9	63	,,	8	488
,,	16	114	,,	15	352
,,	23	119	,,	22	193
,,	30	179	,,	29	139
July	7	201	October	6	96
,,	14	233	,,	13	19
,,	21	375	,,	20	3
,,	28	333			

By the end of May the disease was epidemic in Liverpool, mainly in the north end of the town, but cholera began to appear also in other localities during the second quarter of the year. During the first quarter there were 31 fatal cases; in the subsequent four weeks 23. During the middle of August of that year there were 572 deaths from cholera and 856 from all causes *in one week*. The week ending 18th August was the peak of the cholera epidemic, the number of deaths from this cause declining slowly but progressively in subsequent weeks. The greatest decline occurred in the week ended 22nd September, when the number of

deaths dropped from 352 (in the previous week) down
to 193. Table II shows the deaths from cholera in
each week during the existence of the epidemic.

The occupations of those who died from cholera in
the 1849 epidemic are given in Table III, females and
children being classed under the occupation of the head
of the family:

TABLE III

Class	Deaths
Gentry, Professional Persons, Merchants, etc.	47
Master Tradesmen, Shopkeepers, Clerks, etc.	384
Mechanics and Skilled Labourers, etc.	1,657
Mariners, Pilots, Riggers, etc.	425
Carters, Grooms, etc.	141
Police Officers	32
Customs and Excise Officers	30
Soldiers and Pensioners	37
Servants	30
Hawkers, etc.	38
Porters and Unskilled Labourers, not enumerated	1,861
Unknown	563
Total	5,245

The ages of those who died from cholera were as under:

TABLE IV

Below 1 year	143
1 to 2	158
2 to 5	495
5 to 15	714
15 to 30	887
30 to 45	1,386
45 to 60	953
60 to 70	355
70 to 80	123
80 to 90	26
90 to 100	2
Unknown	3
Total	5,245

Altogether the number of deaths ascribed to cholera registered in the borough of Liverpool in 1849 was 5,245 and from diarrhoea 1,059.[1] The total number of deaths from all causes, according to the tables in the Medical Officer of Health's report for 1849, was 17,047. As the population of Liverpool in that year was not known within any reasonable degree of accuracy it is difficult to translate the figure of total deaths into a crude death-rate; but taking the population of the borough at that time as a little over 300,000, the death-rate would have been in the region of 52 per thousand as compared with 13·5 in 1944. The difference between these figures of 1849 and 1944 is an eloquent tribute to the work of those pioneers in the field of hygiene— of whom Duncan was the first—whose imagination and foresight have so greatly increased the healthiness of our towns.

At the end of his account of the cholera epidemic in his report on the year 1849 Duncan devotes a page and a half to some reflections on the methods of propagation of "fever" and cholera. These expressions of opinion are worth quoting:

The two epidemics of fever and cholera afford some striking points of contrast. First, in their mode of propagation; fever spreading by contagion from district to district, until it covered the whole town; cholera apparently dependent upon atmospheric influences, appearing almost simultaneously in different localities—the one revelling amidst filth and overcrowding; the other, while evincing a decided predilection for such conditions, affording at the same time numerous exceptions to the rule, and attacking individuals and places not generally supposed obnoxious to the attacks of fever: the latter being thus more decidedly than cholera under the control

[1] Cholera was widespread throughout England and Wales in the year 1849. Farr estimated the total number of deaths from cholera and diarrhoea in that year as 72,180.

of Sanatory measures. With regard to age and sex also, there are striking points of difference, in the more equal division of the fever mortality between the sexes, and the more even distribution of the cholera mortality over different periods of life.

The experience of the late epidemic has modified in some measure the opinion generally entertained by the medical profession as to the non-contagious character of the disease. For myself, after much experience of the epidemic during its former as well as its later visit to Liverpool, I am of opinion that while an individual may inhabit with impunity even the same room with a Cholera patient, provided he abstain from absolute contact with the secretions, it is dangerous to handle the body after death or to wash the linen or bedclothes of the deceased. But independently of these conditions—the death of the patient and the coming in contact with the secretions —I know of no instance which supports in any way the theory of contagion. I have already given various examples which support the view now stated. Many more might be adduced, without referring to the numerous cases of hospital carriers and nurses who fell victims to the disease; but I shall confine myself to the following. A Custom-house officer on duty on board a ship where a fatal case of cholera occurred, went home to a distant part of the town, which was entirely free from the disease, sickened and died. His wife also took the disease, and died. No other case occurred in the neighbourhood. A fatal case of cholera occurred in a family residing in Frederick Street. The remaining members of the family removed to lodgings in a court in Duke Street, where the mother died of cholera a day or two after her removal. The landlady of the house, who had nursed her during her illness, died of the disease; which spread no further in the court. But I repeat—however unscientific the opinion may appear—that it is only in case of death, and handling the secretions, that there is any trustworthy evidence of danger to the attendants.

It does not look as if Duncan had seen Snow's pamphlet, *On the Mode of Communication of Cholera*, which was first published in the summer of 1849. It was reprinted in a much enlarged form in 1855. Dr. Snow had had first-hand experience in London of the 1848–9 and 1853–4 epidemics of cholera and his observations had led him to the conclusion that the *materies morbi* in the case of cholera contained a specific micro-organism which was conveyed in the discharge of persons suffering from the disease by the agency of the water supplies. Duncan, in his theorizing on the question, failed to reach any conclusions of value in regard to the mode of communication of cholera. He certainly suspected the secretions and thought it dangerous to handle the body of a cholera patient after death, but he considered that there was no evidence to support the theory of contagion. Only in case of death, in his view, or as a result of handling secretions, was there any trustworthy evidence of danger to the attendants on a case of cholera. Duncan was evidently in two minds about the contagiousness of the disease. When he talked about the danger of handling the patient (but only when dead!) and his secretions he was evidently inclining to the theory of contagion; but at other times he adopted the opinion, generally entertained by the medical profession at that time, that cholera was non-contagious. Duncan further elaborated his opinions on the aetiology of cholera in a letter to Dr. Head, dated the 23rd November, 1853, as follows:

I have much pleasure in replying to your letter of the 19th November. I forward by this post a copy of a report printed two years ago, and and at page 39 of this report you will find my opinion on the question of the contagious or non-contagious nature of cholera. You will observe that I believe the disease to be propagated—as a rule—by some atmospheric

E

influence whose nature is as yet undetermined and which requires some predisposing cause as filth, moisture or overcrowding to call it into action— more particularly in certain stages of the epidemic. The history of cholera outbreaks is conclusive in my opinion, against the idea of contagion being, as a rule, the mode of propagation. But there are exceptional cases which it is difficult to explain on any other supposition than that the disease does, in certain circumstances, become contagious; these instances, however, being so rare and so limited in application (to the nurse or washerwoman where death takes place) as to justify us in considering it practically as non-contagious.

During the last two months we have had about 120 fatal cases of cholera here—fully three-fourths among the foreign immigrants; and amongst these I have certainly met with a larger proportion of "exceptional" cases than I did in the former epidemics. When the disease first broke out at Newcastle I was told that the peculiar feature of the visitation was its appearing by twos and threes in the same house. This, however, by no means proves the contagious nature of the disease; and having been afterwards for some time absent on the Continent I have not heard whether the same peculiarity was noticed throughout.

I consider the diarrhoea which has usually been prevalent along with cholera as essentially the same disease in an early stage. Of course there will be cases of diarrhoea, as there always are, unconnected with the cholera epidemic, but after allowing for these, the excess over the average of the particular season may fairly be set down as cases of the epidemic.

Such being Duncan's views in regard to the aetiology of the disease it is not surprising that when, in August, 1848, he was asked to report on "precautions expedient with reference to the possibility of the cholera appearing in the borough" he should have contented himself with saying that the causes which predisposed to cholera being the same as those which predisposed to other diseases of the zymotic class, no special means of *prevention* were available beyond those which were necessary to improve the sanitary conditions of the town generally; that impure air and moisture had been most generally observed in connection with cholera, and the proper preventive measures in so far as these were within the control of the Committee were effective house and surface cleansing; court and cellar drainage; the drainage, or where impracticable, the filling up, of pools of stagnant water; the systematic removal of middens from courts, and an ample supply of water in the worse-conditioned districts. He suggested also that instructions should be given for a more immediate removal of street sweepings, and for the daily cleansing of the back streets and passages in courts; and that the police and inspectors of scavengers should give notice of midden-steads which required emptying, where the inhabitants had neglected to do so.

In regard to measures of *alleviation* Duncan recommended that provision should be made by the parish authorities for immediate assistance in the early stages of the disease and that hospitals should be provided in different quarters of the town for the accommodation of the destitute and those whom it was inexpedient to treat in their dwellings.

When, in December, 1848, an outbreak of cholera was threatened, additions to the staff of the Inspector of Nuisances were made, under the Medical Officer of Health's advice, by the Health Committee, and it became possible to make additional inspections of those parts of the town where the disease had reached high proportions; the Water Committee arranged for the washing out of the courts in sixty-five streets as often as the limited supplies of water would allow; and notices were served on the owners of houses—during the course of the epidemic—to cleanse the interiors. This cleansing mainly consisted of lime-washing. Later, while the epidemic was in progress, Duncan served notices on owners to lime-wash the exteriors of all court houses which were not open to the street throughout their entire length, in infected and threatened districts. He seemed to be very satisfied that these measures of cleansing had—at least apparently— arrested the progress of the disease. "In so far as I can judge, the exterior lime-washing had, in numerous instances, the most marked and decided effect in reducing the mortality." He gave an example—*post hoc ergo*—of the courts in Oriel Street from which, before the lime-washing, the weekly deaths from cholera were fourteen, but after it were reduced to three per week.

At that time in our history the provision of hospitals devolved upon the Select Vestry in the Parish of Liverpool and upon the Guardians of the West Derby Union in the extra-parochial wards. Early in 1849 a hospital for the reception of cholera patients was opened by the Select Vestry in Queen Anne Street, but as this was situated at an inconvenient distance from the districts where cholera was likely to prevail Duncan appealed to the Vestry to open a hospital situated nearer to the likely source of patients and, after some delays, accommodation was provided in Vauxhall Road. The arrangements for conveying patients to hospital were no doubt inefficient in the extreme, although Duncan gives no information about them in his reports, and distance was therefore an important factor when the collapsed and dehydrated condition of many of the patients is taken into account. Commenting on the factor of distance, he makes the remark that "it has been found that the mortality of patients in cholera hospitals is, *ceteris paribus*, proportioned to the distance of the hospitals from the patients' dwellings." This was also the official opinion of the General Board of Health. As time went on and the epidemic of cholera increased in

violence, the Select Vestry, at Duncan's request, opened
a further hospital in Ansdell Street (on the 20th August)
and in the first week of September a House of Refuge
was opened, but this seems to have been done too late
to be of service. The function of a House of Refuge was
to afford a temporary asylum for those whom it was
thought desirable to remove from houses where cholera
had appeared "until the houses were thoroughly
purified or the *atmospheric poison* [my italics] had passed
away."

One of the extraordinary facts about this epidemic
of 1849, which involved many thousands of cases, is the
small number of patients treated in hospital. A few
patients suffering from cholera were admitted into the
West Derby Fever Hospital in Harper Street and
150 into the Toxteth Park Hospital, but the remaining
hospitalized patients, numbering in all 770 (of whom
407 died), were treated at the three specially opened
parish hospitals—Queen Anne Street, Vauxhall Road
and Ansdell Street. The remaining thousands of
patients stricken with cholera during that year remained
at home, with such medical care as the parish and dispensary doctors—increased in number during the epidemic—could afford them.

An opinion which Duncan entertained about prevention brought him into conflict with the Medical
Relief Committee—a body composed of representatives
of the Borough Council, the Poor Law Guardians and
the Magistrates, appointed specially to deal with the
epidemic. Duncan's view was that, when cholera is
epidemic, a large proportion of the cases are preceded
by diarrhoea which continues for a period varying from
a few hours to several days before passing into cholera.
"As this premonitory diarrhoea is comparatively amen-
able to treatment, the great object is to discover such
cases in the early stages and to arrest them before
merging into confirmed cholera." He therefore prevailed upon the Medical Relief Committee to engage
twenty medical practitioners whose duty it was to visit

daily every house in their respective districts to inquire as to the existence of untreated premonitory diarrhoea or cholera, which, if found, was referred to the ordinary medical officer of the district for treatment. In this way, the report observes, seventy-nine of the most densely peopled streets of the borough, containing about 10,000 houses and probably 80,000 inhabitants—were brought under daily medical inspection during the three months in which this system continued in operation. This team of medical visitors changed the locality of their visits as the epidemic passed from one part of the borough to another, and in this way, as Duncan observes, "A disciplined force of medical combatants thus followed close upon the heels of the enemy in every new position which it occupied." Such arrangements continued for some time, but at the beginning of August, 1849, the Medical Relief Committee, without any previous consultation with Duncan, who was entrusted with the supervision of the house-to-house visitation, resolved to discontinue the system of medical visits to houses and to substitute a visitation by lay persons. The Medical Officer of Health, firmly convinced that this was a wrong system, wrote a strong letter of protest to the Chairman of the Medical Relief Committee in which he said that the first duty of the visitors (i.e. ascertaining the existence of premonitory symptoms) was one which frequently required considerable tact and management, and that even the medical visitors employed, in many instances, failed to elicit the truth because patients had concealed their condition. "If this happens with medical men of education, how much more likely is it to happen with visitors of the class now proposed—their inferiors in education, most probably their inferiors in tact, and not coming recommended by the title 'Doctor,' that usually all-prevailing passport to the houses of the poor!" This protest was unavailing. The Medical Relief Committee saw no reason to modify their decision, and a system of lay visiting was put into effect.

But this arrangement lasted only a short time, as the General Board of Health, on the facts being represented to them (probably by Duncan), issued an order requiring the system of medical visitation to be resumed.

In a letter to a correspondent which is dated the 11th July, 1854, Duncan refers to his difficulties with the Select Vestry. He says:

> For two or three years after our Act came into operation, I had considerable difficulty with the Select Vestry of Liverpool (answering to the Board of Guardians elsewhere) whenever I had to ask them to spend money, but of late they have become rather more reasonable. In the cholera epidemic of 1849 they refused to act on my recommendations until compelled by an Order of the General Board of Health, and even then they took legal advice as to whether they were bound to obey.

Nevertheless, the members of the Select Vestry do not seem to have been as black as, in his more indignant moments, the Medical Officer of Health painted them. At the end of the cholera outbreak of 1849 he received a copy of a resolution of the Vestry thanking him for his services during the epidemic. In his reply, addressed to Mr. Charles Hart, Clerk to the Select Vestry, Duncan says that he would at all times be happy to render the Vestry any service in his power within the scope of his official duties.

The foregoing account of the cholera epidemic of the year 1849 in the borough of Liverpool, as extracted from the Medical Officer of Health's report for that year, is given at some length partly because of its intrinsic epidemiological interest and partly because it illustrates Duncan's methods. When the epidemic began he had been in office for rather more than a year; he possessed no personal staff—not even a clerk; and for hospital accommodation, such as it was, he was entirely dependent upon the resources of the Select Vestry. Confronted by a critical situation, the like of which no modern Medical Officer of Health can conceive, he reacted promptly, courageously and vigorously, mobilizing the scanty resources at his command, and by his leadership inspired the community, each member of which was in grave danger, to renewed efforts. One of Duncan's gravest difficulties, for which he was in no way responsible, was the absence of medical supervision at the Port of Liverpool and the lack of legal powers to prevent the admission of persons travelling by ship from other parts of the United Kingdom and Ireland while suffering from any of the major infectious diseases, or to isolate them until the danger of the transmission of infection was over. Several times, during the early stages of the epidemic, persons came into Liverpool from Edinburgh and Dumfries while actually suffering from cholera, and others arrived in the last stages of the incubation period, falling a victim to the disease within a few hours. Some of these persons came under the notice of the Medical Officer of Health but it is certain that many did not, and that these, entering the community, constituted foci of infection from which radiated numerous cases. Lacking precise knowledge of the mode of transmission of cholera, with insufficient hospital accommodation and inadequate medical staff, in a community which was repeatedly being infected from outside, Duncan was helpless to stay the course of the epidemic of 1849. How it burnt itself out, at this distance of time we cannot say, but presumably the advent of cold weather early in November had the effect of destroying the organism, or perhaps the flies which, to a considerable extent, conveyed it. In that month only two deaths from cholera occurred and throughout the whole of the year 1850 there were only forty-six deaths attributable to this cause, nearly all in the third quarter.

As will be seen from the account of the health of the borough of Liverpool given in Duncan's report for the years 1847–50, the main interest centred upon the epidemics of 1847 and 1849, which were of a most serious and devastating character. No doubt measures to combat epidemic diseases took up the major part of Duncan's time during the first five years of his period of office as Medical Officer of Health of the borough of Liverpool; but the initiation of measures of general sanitation was not neglected even during the epidemic years; at the end of the report the Medical Officer of Health devotes a dozen pages to describing the action which had been taken under the various sections of the Liverpool Sanitary Act, 1846:

The duties indicated by the 122nd clause of the Sanitary Act [he says] are so important that in a town like Liverpool with 370,000 inhabitants—a large proportion of them surrounded by local, removable causes of disease—they might profitably engage the entire services and undivided attention of an Officer of Health. The efficient discharge of these duties obviously requires that, in so far as consistent with his other duties, he should daily visit some portion of the districts inhabited by the poorer classes, with the view of ascertaining the existence and procuring the removal of any local cause of disease which may be found to exist. Those localities in which diseases known to depend upon preventable causes may be prevailing at the time should of course be selected for the purpose. In planning the routine of my duties I proposed that, *in so far as practicable to do so*, I should visit every house in the worst-conditioned districts in which I might find from the Registrars' returns that a death from a *zymotic* disease had taken place, or where from other sources of information I had reason to believe that any zymotic disease was prevalent. As it was impossible to visit every case of this description scattered over a superficies of 5,000 statute acres, I have in the discharge of this portion of my duties given the preference to fever, as being the disease whose connection with local causes has been most distinctly traced, but including where practicable, dysentery, diarrhoea, small pox, scarlatina, etc., when occurring in districts likely to present local causes tending to originate, propagate or aggravate such diseases. By the frequent visitation of such districts by the Officer of Health inspecting not merely the exterior but penetrating into the interior, of the dwellings of the poorer classes—many causes of disease and mortality must be discovered which would otherwise have passed unnoticed.

Previously to the passing of the Sanatory Act, the benefit to be derived from an inspection of the *interior* of the dwellings has been in a great measure overlooked; for there is no doubt that in many cases the preventable causes existing *within*, are even more influential in the production of ill-health than those which exist without, the habitations of the poor, and which thrust themselves more prominently into notice. In the character of *Medical* Officer of Health, I have in almost every instance gained ready access to a house of sickness or where death had recently occurred from a contageous disease, and my advice had been thankfully accepted, where an officer not invested with a medical character might have been denied admission, or his advice more doubtingly received.

This statement of fundamental principles could hardly be bettered. The first principle is that it is important that the poorer districts, especially those in which epidemic diseases prevail, should be frequently visited by the Officer of Health in order that the local causes of such diseases should be removed. Duncan was at the time the only Officer of Health, and accordingly, at times when infectious diseases were prevalent, and especially during epidemics, he visited the threatened districts to the limit of his time and strength. To-day the duties and responsibilities of a Medical Officer of Health have enormously increased and personal visitation of districts as a matter of routine is impracticable. The inspection of the poorer quarter of a town is still as important as it was in Duncan's time but it is now carried out by trained staff, sanitary inspectors and health visitors, and it is done systematically all the year round and not only during the times of epidemics. A Medical Officer of Health in the middle of last century had no trained staff and his field of action was limited accordingly.

In the second place Duncan emphasized the importance of inspecting the *interior* of buildings since in many cases the preventable causes of diseases lie within. If he had had the accumulated experience of his successors he would have realized that many of the preventable causes of diseases—not necessarily infectious diseases—lie within and not outside a dwelling, and if he had followed this line of thought to its logical conclusion he would have arrived at the idea of Personal Hygiene. A step forward such as this could not be expected from a man who was a pioneer in environmental hygiene, and was devoting all his mental and physical energies to solving the immediate and urgent problems of his own time. Duncan's idea that it was a great advantage, in visiting the homes of the poor, to be a medical man, although no longer equally true at the present day with a different type of population, was certainly true of the time at which he was writing. It was a tough, illiterate, drunken population which resided in the industrial districts of the Liverpool of 1850, and only the doctor and the priest could with any safety go among them.

Duncan in his report went on to discuss the sanitary conditions of the schools in the poorer quarters of the borough.

In 1848 [he remarked] I commenced an inspection of the schools connected with the various places of worship in the borough, with the view of ascertaining their arrangements for securing efficient ventilation

—a point on which the health of the scholars so
materially depends. In very few cases indeed did I
find these arrangements satisfactory; although, in
nearly all, the teachers when questioned seemed to
be fully aware of the importance of the subject, some
of them complaining of the injury to their own
health, caused by the air of the room becoming
vitiated after the scholars had been some time
assembled.

He referred in a subsequent paragraph to the
cleansing of filthy houses and mentions that he had
thought it desirable, in the case of the poorest class of
the population, to serve notices upon the owner rather
than upon the occupier—the Act making either party
liable.

Duncan made a number of observations on the important subject of lodging-houses which at that time
frequently housed undesirable members of the population and became centres of infection in the various
epidemics. He was therefore fully aware of the importance of careful inspection and control of these places
and rejoiced when by-laws for the regulation of
lodging-houses came into operation in August, 1848.
The inspectors began their nightly visitations in the
following February.

Up to the end of 1850 [he said] I inspected nearly
1,100 of these houses for which registration had been
required, in order to ascertain the number of lodgers
which each was capable of accommodating with a
due regard to health. Fully nine-tenths of the keepers
are Irish and about 29 per cent. are unable to write.
Experience has shown that few of them can be
depended on for carrying out the Bye-laws, unless
closely watched. This is proved with respect to
overcrowding, by the number of informations laid for
that offence by the Inspectors, which up to the end
of 1849 amounted to 30 per cent. of the whole number
of registered houses. . . . The Bye-law requiring

windows to be opened daily for a certain period is
habitually neglected. . . . With respect to the registered lodging-houses generally, although their condition since registration has been very materially
improved in respect to overcrowding, cleanliness,
ventilation, etc., there is still in regard to many of
them, ample room for improvement.

The last item of any importance in the 1847–50
report refers to cellar dwellings. Duncan says that as
long since as 1802 the late Dr. Currie had called the
attention of the Common Council of Liverpool to the
unhealthiness of these dwellings, but nothing was done
in the matter until forty years afterwards, when (in
1842) the Council obtained power (in the Liverpool
Improvement Act) to prevent the separate occupation
of any cellar less than 7 feet in height, or the floor of
which was more than 5 feet below the level of the
street, or which had not an area of at least 2 feet wide
from 6 inches below the level of the floor to the surface
of the street; and he mentions that the Act of 1842
declared the occupation of cellars in *courts* illegal.
Under the Act about 3,000 cellars had been cleared up
to the end of 1846, but it was found that its provisions
were not sufficiently comprehensive and the Council
accordingly obtained power in the Liverpool Sanitary
Act, 1846, to prevent the separate occupation of any
cellar the floor of which was more than 4 feet below
the level of the street, or which had not an area in
front of not less than $2\frac{1}{2}$ feet in width.

According to the report there were in the borough,
at the time of the passing of the 1846 Act, 14,084
cellars, of which 7,668 were inhabited, with a total
population of nearly 30,000 people. Of the entire number of cellars only about 2,500 could be legally used as
separate habitations under the 1842 and 1846 Acts,
and when the latter Act came into operation on the
1st January, 1847, the clearing of cellars illegally
occupied proceeded rapidly for some months. As this

action appeared to be having the effect of overcrowding the court houses Duncan suggested to the Health Committee that, in order to give time for the supply of new habitations to overtake the demand, not more than 100 cellars a month should be cleared of their inmates. This recommendation was adopted and the result of these operations, up to the commencement of the year 1850, was that upwards of 5,000 cellars had been cleared and 20,000 inmates displaced from them. According to Duncan the cellar population in 1847 formed about 12 per cent. of the entire population of the district, but at the beginning of 1850 it was less than 2 per cent.

Much difficulty had been experienced in carrying out the Act [the Medical Officer of Health reports] from the reluctance of the inmates to leave their miserable abodes, and the expedients to which they have recourse in order to evade the law. Their reluctance seems to be chiefly founded on the convenience offered by the separate entrance to the cellars, and the facilities afforded for selling cakes, fruit, vegetables, chips, etc., and so strong is this feeling that were it not for the constant and systematic inspection of the officers employed for this special purpose under the Inspector of Nuisances, the cellars would be re-occupied nearly as fast as they are cleared.

6

LIVERPOOL CHOLERA EPIDEMIC OF 1854

THE main source of information about the cholera
epidemic of 1854 is contained in one of Duncan's letter-
books which includes all his reports to the General
Board of Health describing the course of the outbreak
and detailing the measures taken to combat it. As a
result of his painfully acquired experience in 1849,
Duncan had arrived at clear ideas as to the steps he
should take to mobilize his resources in the event of
another epidemic. These steps depended almost entirely
on the willing co-operation of the Select Vestry, which
possessed its own Poor Law Institutions and had the
resources necessary to open new hospitals when the
epidemic situation demanded it. In addition, the Select
Vestry had a number of district medical officers and this
staff could be augmented by the engagement of practitioners from the general body of medical men in the
borough; and, as required, doctors could be employed
as house-to-house visitors. The part which the Health
Committee of the Town Council was able to play was
confined to the use of the staff of the Inspector or
Nuisances for visiting the cholera districts and rectify-
ing sanitary defects, the putting into force of arrangements for the lime-washing of the court houses in which
most of the cases of the disease occurred, and the
cleansing of streets and alleys. As the modern system
of notification was not then available, Duncan was
forced to depend upon the house-to-house visitors for
reports of the number of cases and upon the weekly
returns from the registrars for information as to the
total number of deaths. The Health Committee's power
to require owners to lime-wash, cleanse and purify

houses certified by the Medical Officer of Health to be in a filthy or unwholesome condition had been afforded by Section 123 of the Liverpool Sanitary Act, 1846, and this power was extensively used during the epidemic which occurred late in 1854.

In Duncan's correspondence for that year his first fears as to the possibility of an outbreak appear in a letter to the Physician to the South Dispensary complaining that two men living in Brick Street had been attacked by cholera on the 6th January and that the mother of one of them had called at the Dispensary just before midnight and had failed to obtain medical assistance. No further cases appear to have been reported during the early months of the year and towards the end of February there was a formal note from Duncan to the General Board of Health giving the assurance that cholera had disappeared from Liverpool. Late in April there was a letter to the Chairman of the Medical Relief Committee, asking what steps had been taken to provide hospital accommodation "as the season is approaching when another outbreak of cholera becomes probable," and a few days after there was a communication to the Clerk of the West Derby Board of Guardians, asking whether any action had been taken to procure the names of a sufficient number of medical men who would be willing to act as house-to-house visitors if called upon to do so during an epidemic of cholera. He also raised with the Clerk to the Board of Guardians the question of possible arrangements for hospital accommodation.

This year Duncan was evidently determined not to be taken by surprise as he was in the 1849 epidemic when, at the peak of the outbreak, he had repeatedly to press the Select Vestry to provide hospital accommodation for at least a proportion of the large number of cases of cholera which were then occurring. For some time, however, few cases were reported and late in July we find him assuring the foreign consuls in the borough that the epidemic situation in Liverpool was satisfactory. On the 25th July there was a significant reference in a memorandum to the Mayor about an increase of "bowel complaints" due to the higher temperature, in which Duncan said that "during last week sixteen infants died from diarrhoea and five infants and one adult from cholera." In a further letter to the Mayor a few days later he reported that cases of cholera were rather more numerous than was usual at that season of the year, and on 1st August he informed the Chairman of the Medical Relief Committee, Mr. Edward Bradley, that cholera was increasing:

I think it right to let you know that cholera shows a decided tendency to increase. Six fatal cases occurred the week before last and six last week, and several cases have been reported to me yesterday and to-day. We must, of course, expect *some* cholera at this time of the year, but the cases now occurring are much more numerous than in ordinary seasons.

I do not know whether you are aware that the reports of the District Medical Officers reach me only once a fortnight and of course are comparatively useless. I yesterday received the reports for the week ending 19th July—twelve days after the last date. A report of nuisances, under the same date, accompanied the return. If the removal of the nuisances was really important, the delay in transmitting the report might be of serious consequences.

Within the last week I have twice been asked to report to the Mayor, and once to the General Board of Health, on the health of the town and I submit that during the present critical month the District Medical Officers should be required to furnish *daily* reports.

In a further letter to the Chairman of the Medical Relief Committee (1st September, 1854) Duncan said that cholera had increased to such an extent in the Scotland and Vauxhall districts that the arrangements then in force for medical relief were inadequate. It

F

appears that seventy cases had occurred within a few days and that Duncan had himself, while inspecting various districts, discovered several unreported cases, "including two in which death had taken place without any medical attendance." As no reply had been received from the Chairman of the Medical Relief Committee, Duncan wrote on the 5th September to Mr. Charles Hart, the Clerk to the Select Vestry, referring to the rapid increase of the epidemic and the serious responsibility which rested upon him as Medical Officer of Health and expressing the emphatic opinion "that the public safety requires that immediate steps should be taken—if not already adopted—for placing the arrangements for medical relief on such a footing as the urgency of the case required." He informed the Clerk to the Select Vestry that in the preceding week 79 persons had died from cholera in the Parish of Liverpool besides 52 from diarrhoea.

As the epidemic proceeded Duncan was impressed with the need for lime-washing large numbers of courts and alleys and wrote the following letter, dated the 12th September, to the Chairman of the Select Vestry on this and other matters:

It being of great importance that the houses and courts in which cholera may appear should be lime-washed with the least possible delay, and much valuable time being lost by the ordinary mode of serving notice on the owners or occupiers, I have been requested by the Health Committee to suggest to the Select Vestry the propriety of adopting the arrangement which was found so serviceable during the cholera epidemic of 1849, viz. that the Vestry should provide the men and the Health Committee the materials for the work.

During the week ending on Saturday last, 101 deaths from cholera occurred in the *Parish* of Liverpool. The progress of the epidemic is shown by the following numbers which represent the deaths from

cholera in the Parish during the last four weeks
successively, viz., 18, 33, 79, 101. In addition to the
101 cholera deaths during last week, 55 deaths
were caused by diarrhoea. I may add that the deaths
from all causes in the Parish during last week were
305—about double the average mortality, and greater
than in any previous week since the fatal epidemic
of 1849.

I have already been in communication with the
Medical Relief Committee as to the arrangements
which fall within their province, but the steady
increase of the epidemic shows the necessity of
arrangements more commensurate with the exigencies of the case, and which will ensure prompt and
efficient medical attendance to every necessitous
person who may be attacked with cholera or its premonitory symptoms.

On the 15th September he recommended to the
Medical Relief Committee that additional medical
assistance should be provided in two of the worst
districts in order that proper attention should be given
to patients in their homes who were suffering from
cholera, and that hospital accommodation should be
arranged near the infected districts "to prevent the
loss of life which all medical authorities agree in stating
is caused by the removal to a distance of cholera
patients in collapse or in a state approaching collapse."
Near the end of September the number of deaths
registered from cholera in one week had reached the
high figure of 173 but the epidemic was not yet at its
peak. Reporting to the Danish Consul in that month
Duncan said that in the last eight weeks the deaths
from cholera had been successively 9, 23, 21, 21, 39,
85, 113 and 173. He was at this stage of the epidemic
very dissatisfied with the tardy response of the Medical
Relief Committee to his repeated recommendations in
regard to the provision of hospitals and the appointment of additional medical staff for visiting and treat-

ment purposes, and he seemed to feel that his routine attendance at meetings of that committee was a waste of time. He wrote to the Clerk of the Select Vestry accordingly:

These circumstances, with others, have led me reluctantly to the conclusion that my continued attendance at meetings of the Medical Relief Committee is not likely to be productive of beneficial results. I have therefore resolved to withdraw from them for the present unless specially invited to attend, but I shall be at all times ready and willing to give the Committee my best advice and assistance whenever called upon to do so.

In the week ending the 23rd September there were 270 deaths; this proved to be the peak of the epidemic and thereafter the number of weekly deaths from cholera gradually declined. In the following week, ending the 30th September, the number of deaths had dropped to 171. Duncan reported the course of the epidemic since the 29th July, as indicated by the weekly numbers of deaths, to the General Board of Health and ended his letter by criticizing severely the actions (or rather inaction) of the Medical Relief Committee:

In my communication of the 9th September, I stated that the Medical Relief Committee of the Select Vestry doubted the fact of cholera being epidemic here, although in the previous week it had caused 85 deaths, and that I consequently found a difficulty in inducing them to adopt the measures which the state of the public health appeared to me to render necessary. I regret to say that it was not until the 23rd September when the epidemic attained its maximum that the Committee were induced to adopt measures, which although still not in all respects satisfactory, are more in accordance with the exigencies of the case.

In October the weekly number of deaths from cholera declined further and during November there were comparatively few cases, as the colder weather had set in. The last recorded death took place on the 15th November, 1854.

Table V gives the weekly number of deaths from cholera in the seventeen weeks during which the outbreak lasted:

TABLE V

Weekly periods ending on	Number of Deaths
July 29th	9
August 5th	23
,, 12th	21
,, 19th	21
,, 26th	39
September 2nd	85
,, 9th	113
,, 16th	173
,, 23rd	270
,, 30th	171
October 7th	95
,, 14th	59
,, 21st	30
,, 28th	16
November 4th	11
,, 11th	9
,, 18th	1
Total	1,146

The 1854 epidemic was the last but one of the severe cholera outbreaks from which Liverpool suffered in the nineteenth century. From the list of weekly deaths given above it will be seen that the outbreak in 1854 with a total of 1,146 deaths and a peak of 270 deaths in one week was much less serious than the epidemic of 1849 when the corresponding figures were 5,245 and 572.[1] In the 1849 epidemic the peak was

[1] It may be surmised that the work already done since 1847 in the direction of the cleaning up of the borough was already bringing in returns and that the smaller number of cases of cholera in the 1854 outbreak as compared with the one in 1849 was the result of sanitary measures which had by then been put into operation.

reached in the week ending the 18th August, but in 1854 it was much later—in the week which ended on the 23rd September. The height of the epidemic in both years was attained in the season when the prevalence of flies normally reaches a maximum. From the epidemiological point of view the two outbreaks, apart from a pronounced difference in the number of cases, had somewhat similar characteristics, of which the principal was a long slow rise in the weekly returns. In the 1854 outbreak the time which elapsed from the onset to the peak was approximately equal to the time from the peak to the cessation of the epidemic, while in 1849 the period of rise was much longer than the period of fall. Neither in 1849 nor in 1854 was there anything of an explosive character such as was associated with the two water-borne outbreaks in London in 1848–9 and 1853–4, of which Snow writes so graphically. From their characteristics we may therefore infer that the Liverpool outbreaks of cholera were certainly not water-borne, but that the infection was passed on from the cholera patients either by direct contact or by contact with the excretions in bedding and clothing or through the agency of flies. The Liverpool water supply was obtained from deep wells on the outskirts and it is unlikely that they were infected; whereas in the London cholera outbreaks about that time, water was drawn from shallow wells (e.g. Broad Street), or directly from a heavily polluted river. The courses of the epidemics and the modes of infection were thus essentially different in the two towns.[1]

There remains the interesting question as to how cholera was introduced into the borough in 1849 and

[1] No doubt in the London outbreaks a proportion of the cases of cholera were infected through the agency of flies. The following is quoted from Sir Harold Scott's *Some Notable Epidemics*: "Yet another shrewd observation of Dr. Snow. A friend told him that having placed in his room in summer when flies were abundant an infusion of quassia to poison them, he could often taste the bitter quassia on his bread and butter. If then flies could convey quassia infusion from saucer to food, they could as readily transfer fragments of cholera dejecta present on linen." Page 7.

1854. There is little doubt that the infection in these two epidemics of which we have some detailed knowledge, and, by inference, in others, was brought into the Port of Liverpool by immigrants. Duncan seems quite clear in his mind that the 1849 outbreak was introduced into Liverpool by Irish immigrants travelling by way of the Scottish ports and the grave character of this epidemic was increased by repeated new importations of the disease. In regard to the 1854 outbreak the evidence in favour of importation is not so clear. The last known cases of imported cholera occurred in September and early October, 1853, and the victims had arrived from Hamburg and Rotterdam (see pages 91–6). As the cold weather was approaching, little harm was done in the borough by the importation of these cases and only a handful of Liverpool residents were attacked. Before the end of the year this minor epidemic had died down and for a time no known cases of cholera existed in the borough. On the 6th January, 1854, however, two cases of cholera came to Duncan's notice (see page 80), and after that there seems to have been no further cases for several months. It is unlikely, therefore, that the origins of the epidemic which began in July, 1854, can be traced to the importation of cholera from Hamburg and Rotterdam in September and October, 1853. It is hardly possible that the infection from this outbreak or from the two cases which Duncan reports as having occurred in January could have remained hidden in the borough, unknown to the district medical officers and the physicians at the dispensaries, during the whole of the first six months of 1854.

We are forced to come to the conclusion that the 1854 outbreak was due to a fresh importation from the Continent or from Ireland, perhaps early in July, and that the favourable weather in that month enabled the disease to spread rapidly amongst the population in the working-class districts of Liverpool.

The 1854 epidemic and an outbreak in 1866 were the

last serious visitations of cholera which occurred in
Liverpool, and it is interesting to consider whether the
sanitary improvements effected in the borough by the
Town Council since the passing of the Liverpool Sanitary Act of 1846 had had the effect of rendering conditions unfavourable for the propagation of the disease.
If the epidemic had been water-borne and a pure water
supply had later been provided there would be no
difficulty in reaching the conclusion that the cessation
of outbreaks had been due to the substitution of pure
for polluted water. But such a simple conclusion is not
possible in the various Liverpool outbreaks if it is
accepted that the spread of the disease was due to case-
to-case infections and not to the ingestion of polluted
water. The method of spread of cholera by case-to-case
infection is not a usual or favourable one and it would
require exceptional circumstances for the occurrence of
a large epidemic by this means. These exceptionally
favourable circumstances for case-to-case infection
were undoubtedly present in Liverpool in the fifth and
sixth decades of last century—a poor population with
low standards of living and of cleanliness, existing
under conditions of appalling overcrowding in courts
and cellars which possessed hardly any of the rudiments
of sanitation. Even in such circumstances the outbreaks
of cholera were of relatively small dimensions except
in 1849, when repeated reinfections from outside took
place. It might be expected, therefore, that a comparatively small improvement in the sanitary circumstances
of the working-class districts of Liverpool, especially in
regard to the sanitary disposal of excreta, would turn
the balance against the transmission of the disease,
and that, although small outbreaks arising from imported cases might occur, the circumstances of the
borough were no longer so favourable for the occurrence of a large epidemic. This is what seems to have
happened. The efforts of the Corporation between
1846 and 1866 effected a marked reduction in the
population living in cellars, and with lodging-houses

placed under strict supervision made it less likely that they would continue to be the breeding places from which epidemics of infectious diseases made their way into the remainder of the borough. Under the provisions of the Liverpool Building Act, 1842, and the Liverpool Sanitary Act, 1846, private building was subject to control. It was no longer permitted to build, without let or hindrance, houses in narrow courts with only the most primitive sanitary accommodation. As the two decades under discussion were a period of intense building activity it was highly beneficial that the Town Council through its Health Committee had received statutory powers to remove some of the worst sanitary evils from which the borough was suffering, and to prevent them from being perpetuated in the new areas then being rapidly developed. So the old districts had their sanitary standards raised and the newly built areas, into which many of the inhabitants of the older houses removed, provided from year to year additional living accommodation which was superior to the older types of houses. In both old and new housing areas there were higher standards of sanitation and cleanliness—improved scavenging, the paving of courts and alleys, an increased water supply and better facilities for washing the streets. All these improvements were initiated between the years 1842 and 1866 and further developments took place as the century wore on. But it seems as if, after 1866, enough had been done to turn the scales against the cholera epidemics which had up to that time caused so many deaths and inflicted so much suffering amongst the population of Liverpool.

7

ANNUAL REPORTS OF THE HEALTH OF LIVERPOOL, 1851–60

A BRIEF résumé of some of the salient points in the remaining annual reports is all that is necessary. In the 1852 report Duncan permitted himself to boast that, for the second time since the Registration Act came into operation, the mortality of Liverpool, in that year, was less than that of Manchester. From diseases of the zymotic class the deaths were 3,503, i.e. 1,268 less than the average mortality from this cause in the four years 1848–51. Evidently the work done—mainly by the Borough Engineer—under the Liverpool Sanitary Act, 1846, of which some account will be given later, was beginning to show some returns. "Sudden and Violent Deaths" were 490, of which 8 were murders, 8 manslaughters, and 98 ascribed to the "Visitation of God." Forty-eight deaths were registered as having been caused by the direct effects of intemperance, viz. 26 from delirium tremens and 22 from the more immediate consequence of excessive drinking. At the end of the report Duncan, in a letter to medical practitioners on the subject of death certificates, referred to the Sanitary Act of 1846 and expressed the hope that at no distant period an amended Act would be passed. (This hope was fulfilled in 1854 by the passage of the Liverpool Sanitary Amendment Act.)

The year 1853 was rendered noteworthy by the occurrence of a small outbreak of cholera imported mainly from Germany through Hamburg. A copy of the letter in which this outbreak was reported by Duncan to the General Board of Health is available in the Public Health Department's letter-books of that year and it is given here as an example of his official style. By 1853 Duncan had persuaded the Town Council to appoint a deputy, but he appears to have had little clerical assistance and all official correspondence was conducted by him.

The letter, dated the 8th October, 1853, is as follows:

Understanding on my return home after an absence of some weeks that no formal report had been made of the cholera cases which have lately occurred here, I think it right to forward for the information of the General Board of Health the following statement of facts, chiefly supplied to me (in so far as they refer to occurrences up to the 3rd instant inclusive) by my Deputy, Dr. Cameron, who acted for me during my absence.

It will be observed that nearly all the cases have been those of emigrants recently arrived from Germany.

The first case occurred on the 30th August, the patient being a Danish emigrant, *æt.* twenty-five, in good circumstances, who arrived here a day or two previously from Hamburg where he had remained about a fortnight. He had been attacked with diarrhoea on the day after leaving Hamburg. He died on the 31st, twenty hours after the development of cholera symptoms.

The second and third cases were also those of an emigrant and his wife from Hamburg, who were attacked the 4th September, a few hours after arrival and died on the 7th and 5th. They lodged in the same house in which Case No. 1 died, in Duke Street, a healthy situation. No other cases have occurred in this house.

The fourth and fifth cases were those of a child attacked immediately after its arrival from Rotterdam and died the 4th September and its mother attacked next day and died the 6th September. Two others of the family had severe diarrhoea, but recovered.

6. A woman from Hamburg, ill on arrival, died the 5th September. Another of the family had died in Hull after landing there.

7. A child from Hamburg, taken ill and died the 13th September, four days after arrival.

8. A German, *æt.* fifty, from Hamburg (had only been three or four hours there on his way from Mecklenburg) attacked the day after arriving here and died on the 23rd September.

9. A man, *æt.* twenty-four, from Hamburg, took ill two days after arriving and recovered.

10. An infant, eight months old, from Hamburg, seized the day after arrival, and died the 24th September.

11. A child, three and a half years, from Hamburg, took ill two days after arriving, and died the 24th September.

12. A woman, *æt.* thirty, from Rotterdam, attacked the day after arrival, and died the 25th September.

13. A woman, *æt.* twenty-nine, from Hamburg, took ill three days after arrival and recovered.

The whole of the foregoing had come to Liverpool by way of Hull.

14. A child from Rotterdam direct (by screw steamer *Pelican* on board of which a passenger had died at sea from cholera) sent to hospital 27th, and died the 30th September. The father and mother had choleraic diarrhoea, but recovered.

15. An English emigrant, *æt.* forty-five, died the 29th September, half an hour after admission into the hospital from the *William Tipscott* on board of which he had been for six days with a number of German emigrants.

No other case was known to have occurred in this ship.

In addition to the above, many emigrants had suffered from diarrhoea more or less severe during the period in question.

The *Silas Greenman* emigrant ship went into the river the 21st September. She had about 400 passen-

gers, chiefly Germans, but a good many English
and a few Irish. Some came on board . . . the 25th
and a few cases of diarrhoea occurred, the second
being an Englishman, suffering among others. On
the night of the 25th September one of the passengers' cooks, an Irishman who had been drinking
freely before coming on board, was attacked with
cholera and died next day. About the same time
another Irishman, also a passengers' cook, and
occupying the same berth with the former, was
taken ill. He was sent ashore next day and recovered.
On the 27th, 28th and 29th six passengers died.
About fifty in all, chiefly Germans, were affected
with diarrhoea as also three or four of the crew,
exclusive of those mentioned. The cooks' berth was
close to the ship's bows, and from thence the disease
travelled along the same side of the vessel to about
midships, then crossed over and continued its course
down the opposite side. On the 30th September and
1st October, the whole of the passengers were
landed and the greater number sent to the Emigrants'
Home in Moorfields—a large house capable of
accommodating 300 people, and which has been
taken by the Parish Authorities for three months, to
be used in the meantime as a House of Refuge. On
these two days, five more deaths occurred, and from
the 2nd to the 6th inclusive, twenty more, making
thirty-two in all. The mortality seems now to be
arrested. The passengers are inspected daily and
every case of diarrhoea at once transferred to the
Workhouse hospital.

On the 4th instant, the *Isaac Wright* emigrant ship
which had sailed a fortnight previously, returned to
this port, having experienced very stormy weather,
during which her passengers (530 in number) had
been exposed to great privations. About fifty deaths
had occurred among them, and most of these probably from cholera and diarrhoea. The whole of the
passengers were landed at once, the sick (about
thirty) sent to the Parish Hospital, and nearly all the

healthy (380) to wards in the Workhouse which had been prepared for such an emergency by drafting off the children to the Industrial School at Kirkdale.[1] These wards were capable of accommodating 750 persons. Some of the passengers in better circumstances and in apparent good health, were allowed to go to private lodgings. Three deaths occurred within an hour after landing, and during the four following days (up to the present time) thirteen more fatal cases have been added to the list. There remain under treatment from among the passengers of the two ships, thirty-six cases of diarrhoea and cholera.

In the meantime several fatal cases of cholera had occurred among the residents of the town. The first suspicious case was that of an Irish labourer in full employment, living in a clean and not overcrowded house in a well-conditioned street in a healthy part of the town. He was attacked on the 12th September and died the 15th (it is said) without premonitory diarrhoea. On the 26th a child five years old, was taken ill in a densely peopled street (Sparling Street) and died on the 30th September, on which day the mother was also attacked and died on the 1st October. The fourth indigenous case was that of an Irish oyster-seller, *æt.* forty, residing in a court in Lace Street, one of the worst streets in Liverpool, who was taken ill on the morning of the 27th September and died on the evening of the same day. The fifth case was also that of an Irishman, *æt.* forty-five, in extremely destitute circumstances, residing in a court in Milton Street, attacked the 3rd October and died next day. The death of a child, *æt.* four, was registered as having taken place from English cholera on the 25th September.

In addition to the above, a few suspicious cases have been reported, none of which have proved fatal, not more than five or six in all.

After the issuing of the instructions of the General

[1] Now Kirkdale Homes.

Board of Health, the 21st September, a Joint Committee, composed of members of the Health Committee of the Council, of the Select Vestry of the
Parish of Liverpool, and of the West Derby Board
of Guardians—was appointed to take the necessary
measures to meet an outbreak of epidemic cholera
whenever it might occur.

The first meeting of the Committee was held on
the 28th September. A considerable addition has
been made to the staff of the Inspector of Nuisances,
with the view of making a thorough and systematic
house-to-house inspection, internal as well as external, in the more densely peopled districts of the
town; extra scavenging and cleansing has been
ordered in the streets occupied by the working
population; and such courts as seem to require it are
washed out from time to time by hoses from the mains.

The Parish Authorities have provided hospital
accommodation for 300 patients in the Workhouse
and have appropriated, as already stated, wards
capable of receiving 750 emigrants or others, whom
it may be considered at any time expedient to
remove. They have also taken a house fitted up for
300 patients, which may be used as a hospital if
required, and are looking out for further hospital
accommodation at the north end of the town, where
cholera may be expected chiefly to prevail. Four
dispensaries have been provided in different districts
of the town, and some of these are now ready. The
names of about thirty medical practitioners have
been received, who are ready to act as House-to-
House Visitors, whenever called upon to do so. The
District Medical Officers report daily all nuisances
or other removable cases of disease which come under
their observation.

The District Medical Officers also report daily the
new cases of diarrhoea presenting themselves, and
from these reports as well as from the returns of
deaths as reported by the Registrars, it does not

appear that any unusual amount of diarrhoea at
present prevails. The deaths from diarrhoea during
last week were 10, the average of the same week of
1848, '50, '51 and '52, being 21. The mortality from
this disease has gradually declined, the deaths in the
last four weeks having been 52, 30, 25 and 19.

I shall continue to report, for the information of
the General Board of Health, any new cases which
may occur.

Gaps in the letter are parts which have not been
copied or cannot be deciphered.

The cholera epidemic which was the main feature of
the health situation in the borough in the year 1854
has already been described in Chapter 6. This visitation
possesses an added interest because it led to acri-
monious correspondence between Duncan and the
Medical Relief Committee. A long printed report on
this dispute, presented by the Medical Officer of Health
to the General Board of Health late in 1854, sum-
marizes the whole of the course of the discussion
between Duncan, the Medical Relief Committee (an
old enemy in the 1849 epidemic) and the General
Board of Health, and contains some of the letters which
passed between the parties.

One of the contentions of the Medical Relief Committee was that they could not discover any legislative
authority making it the province of the officer of health
"to point out to the Committee such curative measures
as he may deem necessary in times of epidemic."
Duncan's reply to this was that early in the epidemic
of 1849, his attention was called by the General Board
of Health to the fact that among the duties prescribed
for him by Act of Parliament was that of "pointing
out the best means of arresting the progress of epidemic
disease" and that he was asked for a statement of the
measures which he had recommended to the Parish
authorities with reference to the epidemic which had
then commenced. "Subsequently," Duncan says, "I was
asked by the Superintending Inspector of the Board to

sign with him, in the discharge of the duties entrusted
to us, a joint representation to the Medical Relief
Committee as to various matters which demanded their
serious and immediate attention."

Dr. Duncan then went on to criticize the Medical
Relief Committee for neglecting to take action in regard
to certain recommendations made by him to them,
which included the provision of an additional hospital
convenient to the cholera districts, the furnishing of
more assistance to the medical officers of those districts,
the appointment of more house-to-house visitors (who, in
the 1849 epidemic, he had recommended should be medi-
cally qualified) and, lastly, the establishment of a medical
practitioner, day and night, at the Cheapside Dispensary.
He included in his report a diagram which shows that
house-to-house visitation, under the control of the
Medical Relief Committee, was not in active operation
until the 1849 epidemic of cholera was on the decline.
It was in fact nearly three weeks too late. Duncan later
on referred to some charges brought by the Medical
Relief Committee against the Health Committee but
said that they had been satisfactorily disposed of.
Referring the report on this dispute to the General
Board of Health, Duncan took the rather extreme step
early in 1855 of writing a personal letter to the President of the Board of Health, which is here reproduced:

Dr. Duncan takes the liberty of forwarding to
Sir Benjamin Hall the accompanying printed remarks
on a letter recently addressed by the Medical Relief
Committee of the Parish of Liverpool to the General
Board of Health.

The Board's letter of the 6th December to the
Medical Relief Committee has been made use of to
convey the impression that the Officer of Health had
unnecessarily stepped out of his province in making
the recommendations which he reported to the Board
on the 7th October, and that his Report to the Board
conveyed an erroneous statement of the facts as they
occurred.

G

Dr. Duncan has felt it necessary, therefore, in his own vindication to print his original report accompanied with remarks on the reply of the Medical Relief Committee. If Sir Benjamin Hall will do Dr. Duncan the favour to peruse these remarks (which occupy the first part of the pamphlet) Dr. Duncan feels confident that the perusal will remove from the President's mind any impression he may have entertained that the Report of the 7th October misrepresented the facts of the case.

Dr. Duncan begs to apologize for this intrusion on Sir Benjamin's time and to say that his only object is to set himself right with the President of the General Board of Health.

The remainder of the report is taken up by the inclusion of a copy of a long letter, dated the 7th October, 1854, from the Public Offices, Cornwallis Street, addressed by the Medical Officer of Health to the Secretary of the General Board of Health. This letter, which is too long to quote here, is devoted mainly to correspondence passing between Duncan on the one hand and the Chairman of the Medical Relief Committee and the Clerk to the Select Vestry on the other. This correspondence contains Duncan's recommendations for action during the epidemic and includes a number of complaints that certain recommendations had not been put into effect. The interesting sequel to Duncan's report of the 7th October to the General Board of Health was his receipt of a letter from that Department a few days after, which contained the following paragraph: "I am to convey to you the thanks of the President for your important and interesting communication, and to state that what you have done has his entire approval." Duncan was quite evidently in high favour with the General Board of Health at that time.

The last three reports which are available—for 1858, 1859 and 1860—are slightly larger than the earlier ones but they still are primarily concerned with death returns. Deaths from zymotic diseases were exceptionally high in the year 1858—4,265. Of these, scarlatina caused 1,187 deaths, measles 524, whooping-cough 496, and diphtheria 62. It is interesting to note the reversal of fatality in those days compared with now as between scarlet fever and diphtheria.[1] In the 1860 report typhus was given as the cause of 562 deaths, and this was less than the average of the preceding years; and 4,053 deaths were ascribed to diseases of the lungs (with consumption). Consumption was at that time excessively fatal in Liverpool with an average annual mortality of about 6 per 1,000 of the population. The size of this annual report is increased by some pages which are devoted to a controversy with Dr. Greenhow,[2] and to a protest against a statement, unfavourable to Liverpool, in the third quarterly report of the Registrar-General for 1858. Greenhow, in a report to the Board entitled *Papers relating to the Sanitary State of the People of England*, had thrown some discredit upon the sanitary condition of Liverpool and upon the efforts made to improve it. It appears that there were statistical fallacies in the report and Dr. Duncan is at pains to point them out.

[1] Diphtheria was in the middle years of last century a disease of little Public Health importance. It had been described by Fothergill in London in 1748 and later by Starr of Liskeard as a clinical entity, and the brilliant work of Brétonneau in the third decade, mainly directed towards proving the specificity of certain infectious diseases, had placed the diagnosis of diphtheria on a sound basis. In Duncan's day, therefore, this disease was known in some quarters, but its occurrence in Liverpool was by no means frequent even in the most overcrowded quarters of the borough. In the annual report for the year 1860, Duncan observes about diphtheria that "this disease, which made its first appearance in Liverpool (if it be a new disease) about three years ago, has not as yet assumed an epidemic character, the deaths having been, in the three years successively, 62, 65, and 58."

[2] Dr. E. H. Greenhow (1814–88) studied medicine at Edinburgh and at Montpelier, and after practising in partnership with his father in North Shields and Tynemouth settled in London in 1853. Greenhow was appointed Lecturer in Public Health at St. Thomas's Hospital in 1855 where, according to Simon, his course was the first of its kind in this country. He frequently reported on epidemiology and public health to the General Board of Health and the Privy Council and served on several Royal Commissions.

In the first place [he says] Greenhow takes the
mortality of a *portion* of the borough, and that the
most unhealthy portion, and represents it as the
mortality of "Liverpool." . . . Secondly, having taken
the most unhealthy portion of the borough, he next
selects a most unhealthy period, within which he
confines his calculations of mortality—a period of
six years (1849–54) the first and last of which were
signalized by visitations of epidemic cholera, increasing the mortality of Liverpool in these two
years alone by upwards of 7,000 deaths.

It is a little difficult to follow Duncan in the second
of these two arguments. Surely it was the duty of the
sanitary authority to protect the community against
cholera. Duncan was of course aware that his efforts
were all but unavailing against the "visitation" of
cholera. But he might equally well have claimed to
deduct deaths from measles, consumption, scarlatina
and typhus from his mortality returns since he was
unable to control them either!

Duncan seemed more than usually perturbed about
Dr. Greenhow's criticisms of Liverpool's mortality,
and in some of his letters referring to this subject
he goes nearer to displaying impatience than in any
other part of the correspondence. Thus in October,
1859, he writes to a friend at the General Board of
Health as follows:

I will send you what reports I can lay my hands
on but to-day I have only time to say that I think
Dr. Greenhow very wrong (if he is really right as
to the mortality of "Liverpool") to whisper his
defence into the ears of his friends in place of making
it as public as my statement (which I repeat) that he
takes the mortality of the most unhealthy portion of
the borough and calls it the mortality of "Liverpool." If he really means to persist in his statement
he will have forfeited all claims to mercy.

On the former occasion he erred through ignorance;
now he sins against the light. I sent him a printed

copy of my report six months ago—why has he kept silence till now? and why does he *now* even venture only to speak in whispers?

And again, early in December, to the same correspondent:

Dr. Greenhow's charge of deception about the mortality of the Parish . . . being compared with the borough now, is too serious to be whispered in corners. He should speak manfully out if he has anything to say. The argument about the excessive proportion of young adults is borrowed from Dr. Farr, who promised me a copy of his calculation on the subject but failed to send it.

Even on Dr. Farr's showing the mortality of the Parish has been reduced four per 1,000, or 1,100 per annum; so that we have saved more lives in ten years than have been lost in battle in the last forty; and yet you theorists turn up your noses at such results.

As to the high district death rates I mentioned at Bradford that in one (Irish) district the death rate had been as high as 50 per 1,000 but was last year only 36½—the highest rate. This year I believe it will not exceed 30; and the Parish 28.

Cesspools, etc. We only obtained power to deal with these five years ago, and our powers are limited and opposed on every side. But you are dissatisfied that only 20 per cent. of all the cesspools in Liverpool have been done away with in that period. Verily some people have a large digestion.

The controversy with Dr. Greenhow continued intermittently until June of 1861 and Duncan appears to have felt that Liverpool had been unfairly criticized both in regard to the mortality rate and to the efforts which the borough had made since 1847 to rid itself of many of the more serious of the sanitary evils from which it had suffered. He was tired of the subject, however, as the following extracts from a letter to the same correspondent as above show:

Liverpool has been unjustly treated. Whatever the

cause may be there seems to be an understanding among the London men to snub Liverpool whenever an opportunity offers and I believe the cavillers would still carp and cavil and object and try to make it appear that we had done nothing even though the Health Committee or its Chairman should write the paper you desire.

Enough has already been said and written to convince those who are open to conviction, and for myself I must remain satisfied with the *mens sibi conscia recti*, and the knowledge that we have done our duty in our generation.

The other subject for controversy arose out of a statement in the quarterly report of the Registrar-General in which the amount of sanitary improvement in Liverpool was unfavourably contrasted with the result of sanitary measures in Ely. It was admitted that "much good has been done" in Liverpool and that "thousands of lives have been saved"; but it was asked "why should not the mortality be as low as that of Ely?" Duncan really let himself go about this.

Ely [he retorted] is situated on an eminence and consists of one principal street with several smaller branching off on either side; having (in 1851) 6,176 inhabitants, most of whom are engaged in agricultural pursuits. Anyone acquainted with Liverpool, and hearing this description of Ely, will be at no loss to see abundant reasons why it should be impossible that any means within the compass of human ingenuity, aided by the most lavish expenditure, can ever succeed in placing the two towns on the same level in respect of mortality.

If Duncan has given a correct impression of the Registrar-General's criticism of Liverpool's sanitary progress, one cannot but feel that the point made in the quarterly report was a stupid one and that the official who wrote the comment had little appreciation of the gigantic efforts which were being made in that large and cosmopolitan borough to improve environ-

mental conditions. The difficulties confronting Newlands, the Borough Engineer, and Duncan, the Medical
Officer of Health, during the years following the
passage of the Liverpool Sanitary Act, 1846, were
enormous and only men of exceptional courage and
devotion could have faced and overcome so many of
them. Looking back on that period from the vantage
point of nearly a century's further experiences one can
more closely estimate at its true worth the work of
these two pioneers who attempted to change an insanitary environment into a sanitary one within the space
of a few years. It was an impossible task—the task of a
century rather than of a score of years, and in Liverpool
and all the large towns in this country the task is not
even yet half completed.

Duncan's annual report for the year 1860 had little
of importance to relate. It began on an optimistic note.
"The mortality of Liverpool has now for two con-
secutive years been lower than in any similar period
hitherto recorded." By now the effects of the machine
age were beginning to tell upon the health of the
inhabitants of the Lancashire towns and Duncan pointed
out with some complacency that the mortality of
Liverpool in 1860 was less than that of Manchester
and Salford, Chorlton, Bolton, Blackburn, Ashton and
Oldham, Preston, Rochdale and Wigan. Duncan, in
this report, expressed some views on a subject which
he had not discussed before, viz. the relationship
between infantile mortality and the birth-rate.

There is no doubt [he wrote] that they exert a
mutual reaction. In a population not otherwise
increasing than by excess of births over deaths, and
where the death-rate is uniform, the deaths of children will decrease in proportion to the decrease of
births, i.e. the fewer the children born, the fewer will
die; but, on the other hand, it may be taken as an
invariable rule—the result of physiological causes—
that where the mortality of infants at the breast is
low, there is a proportionately low birth-rate.

8

SANITARY IMPROVEMENTS IN LIVERPOOL
BETWEEN 1847 AND 1868

Some account has already been given of the sanitary
state of the borough of Liverpool during the first half
of last century when population was rapidly increasing
and the building of houses, uncontrolled by law or
regulation, was proceeding at a pace which was insufficient to provide for the expanding needs of a growing
community. Out of those conditions arose the sanitary
evils of that day—filthy and unventilated court houses
and cellars, overcrowding, the lack of sewerage and
drainage, of adequate arrangements for refuse collec-
tion and of paving for the streets and alleys of the
working-class districts.

Early in the century the gross sanitary evils existing
in Liverpool had been condemned by medical practitioners, by the Health of Towns Commission and in the
report of the Poor Law Commission. Up to 1822 the
paving and sewering of the borough were in the hands
of the Town Council but in that year responsibility was
vested in Commissioners who, in 1829, instructed
Mr. Foster, the Town Surveyor, to report on the
measures required to provide an efficient sewerage
system. In 1830 the Commissioners began to carry out
the works and in ten years they had completed twenty
miles of sewers. The borough was rapidly growing,
however, and this amount was only a small fraction of
the mileage required. Under powers obtained in 1842
the Commissioners constructed a further ten miles of
sewers. But, it is to be noted, these sewers were for
surface water only; it was forbidden to connect house

drains to them. Thus, in 1842, Liverpool was to all intents and purposes unsewered and undrained, and houses were still dependent upon the insanitary and dangerous privy-middens.

According to a paper by Mr. James Newlands, the Borough Engineer, entitled *Liverpool Past and Present in relation to Sanitary Operations*, read to the Public Health Section of the National Association for the Promotion of Social Science in October, 1858, it appears that in 1842 the number of scavengers employed in the parish (or Old Municipal Borough) was only sixty-five, and this force was totally inadequate to keep clean the extent of streets under their charge.[1] Newlands estimated that in the same year the cellar population of Liverpool was about 45,000, and expressed the view that nearly one-half of the labouring population of the borough lived a miserable existence. And he added:

Having then glanced at the progress of sanitary matters . . . we arrive at the period when the publication of a masterly report by Dr. Duncan, our present Medical Officer of Health (presumably the paper read to the Literary and Philosophical Society in 1843 and printed in pamphlet form), stirred the authorities of Liverpool, and the report of Mr. Chadwick, on the condition of the poor, roused all England from its death sleep. Immediately succeeding it the Commission on the Health of Towns published the result of its labours, and the public began to see that much of the misery, the moral degradation, the death and the crime of the land were preventible. The incubus of ignorance was removed and action in a right direction became possible.

As a result of the agitation which had been going on in Liverpool for the improvement of sanitary conditions the Liverpool Sanitary Act of 1846 was passed. Mr. Newlands described it as the first Sanitary Act in the

[1] By 1858 the number of scavengers employed by the Health Committee had increased to 333.

kingdom. It is, however, one thing to obtain powers
in an Act of Parliament and quite another thing to use
those powers. The Liverpool Town Council, to its
credit, acted promptly; it appointed a Medical Officer
of Health and Borough Engineer, under powers con-
ferred by the Act, and instructed the Borough Engineer
to begin operations for the sewerage and drainage of
the town, for which function the Council was now,
under the new legislation, the authority. We are fortunate in possessing the printed reports in which Newlands communicated to the Health Committee of the
borough the successive stages of the great engineering
works necessary to complete the sewering of the town.
The reports refer to each main sewer by a number,
give a list of the streets which it traverses, and include
information about the length of each part of the sewer
and the average cost "per lineal yard," which depended,
inter alia, on the size of the sewer and generally worked
out at between £1 and £2 per yard. Newlands' progress reports cover the periods from 1847 to 1868. His
report which initiated this great scheme was presented
to the Health Committee in 1848. "The Council," he
wrote, "startled by the magnitude of the proposed
work, deliberated long, but eventually gave it their
sanction, and from that time the work has been steadily
carried on."

Under the scheme, taking the datum line as the year
1847, when the Sanitary Act came into operation, to
the year 1858, 80 miles of sewers were constructed
together with 66 miles of "main drains," a total length
of sewers and drains of 146 miles. Included in the work
was the construction of the main outlet sewer which is
six miles long and, for a great part of its length, six
feet high and four feet wide. As the sewers were laid
house drains were constructed and connected with the
sewers.

Other sanitary improvements were made in this
period. By-laws were established providing, in the
case of new dwelling-houses, for a certain amount of

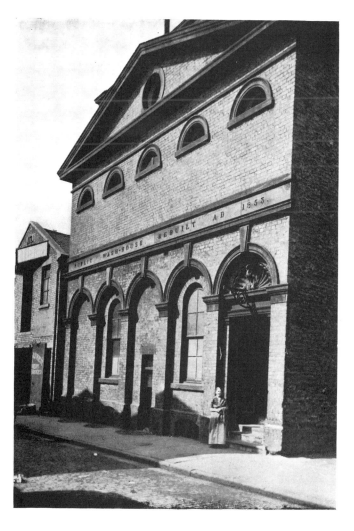

UPPER FREDERICK STREET, BATHS AND
WASH-HOUSE

cubic space in the apartments and a minimum of area in the court yards, a minimum of size for windows in the apartments, and for the proper arrangement of ashpits and conveniences. Baths and wash-houses were erected by the Council.[1] Large numbers of persons were removed from cellars, healthy habitations being simultaneously provided for the displaced population; the paving of streets, alleys and courts was much improved; scavenging was more efficiently performed; water hydrants were multiplied so as to afford greater facilities for washing courts, passages and streets; by-laws for the regulation of slaughter-houses were made and enforced; public conveniences were erected; habitable cellars were registered and put under control; arrangements were made for the proper emptying of ashpits; noxious manufactures and stores, where injurious to health, were dealt with; knackers' yards were placed under control; the nuisance from smoke was abated; and interment in pits was prevented, and eventually intramural burial was abolished or regulated.

This was truly the Golden Age of sanitation. Although the account given above is extracted from Newlands' paper, much of the sanitary work which he details was initiated in Duncan's department, and, indeed, these two officials, whose work was so closely connected, appear to have worked together harmoniously and co-operatively. In his first progress report, covering the period from the 1st January, 1847, to the 31st December, 1850, Newlands observes in an introductory paragraph, "They have generally selected for execution such works as, in the opinion of the Medical Officer of Health, would most effectively contribute to remove the causes of disease, and the results have

---

[1] The provision of public wash-houses, in which Liverpool was a pioneer, is associated with the name of Catherine Wilkinson who, coming from a poor home, drew attention to the need for facilities of this kind during the cholera outbreaks of 1832 and 1834. Mrs. Wilkinson and her husband were appointed the superintendents of the first public baths and wash-house in this country, opened in 1842 in Upper Frederick Street. The Baths and Wash-houses Act was passed in 1846.

abundantly justified this course of procedure."[1] Many
of the sanitary duties detailed above were performed
by the Inspector of Nuisances (Mr. Fresh) and his staff.
Some of the Inspector of Nuisances' reports—addressed
directly to the Health Committee—are available. The
first covers the period from the 1st January, 1847, to
the 31st March, 1851, and it appropriately begins by
detailing the more important duties of the office, which
are: the inspection and suppression of nuisances; the
improvement of the cleansing of filthy and unhealthy
dwellings in the low and crowded districts of the town;
the superintendence of the arrangements necessary for
the removal of middens; the regulation of cellar occupation; the adoption of proceedings necessary to prevent the emission of smoke; the keeping of a slaughter-
house registry; the conducting of a registry of lodging-
houses; and the inspection of cemeteries, knackers'
yards, etc.

As regards nuisances, Fresh was not only acting
under the Liverpool Sanitary Act of 1846, but later
under two general Acts—the Nuisances Removal and
Diseases Prevention Act, 1848, and the Nuisances
Removal and Diseases Prevention Amendment Act,
1849, and this legislation provided ample powers to
deal with the sanitary circumstances of the borough in
an effective way. As an interesting administrative point
Fresh mentioned that:

With the view of promoting unity of action in all
departments under the Health Committee, a daily
communication and co-operation has been established
between the Town Clerk, the Medical Officer of
Health, the Borough Engineer, the Building Surveyor, the Water Engineer, the Head Constable,

[1] From time to time pressure was exerted on the officials to give
priority in regard to the construction of sewers to some of the better-
class districts. Duncan was well aware, as was Newlands, that it was
better policy from the health point of view to sewer and drain as early
as possible the thickly populated industrial quarters of the borough;
and this appears to have become, in the main, the settled practice of the
Health Committee.

and the Inspector of Nuisances, relative to the prevention, suppression and abatement of nuisances, as
well as upon other matters generally affecting the
duties of their several departments. . . .

This report bears a strong likeness to reports of
Chief Sanitary Inspectors at the present day, but compared with his modern successors Mr. Fresh laboured
under the great disadvantage of having no trained
inspectors.

The training and certification of sanitary inspectors
and other members of the staff of a Public Health
Department did not come until nearly half a century
later. Fresh had therefore to appoint such men as he
was able to get and train them himself. In dealing with
cellar dwellings he adopted the wise expedient of
selecting "four intelligent and competent police officers
(being practical tradesmen)" for the purpose of making
an "extensive and special survey," including measure-
ments, of these undesirable habitations.

Many of the improvements in environmental hygiene
which took place in Liverpool in the years following the
passing into law of the Sanitary Act would have proved
impracticable if the Town Council had not taken energetic action to increase the water supplies. It was
realized at an early stage that the cleanliness of the
borough, and therefore the health of the borough,
depended upon copious supplies of water, and as the
scheme for the sewering and drainage of the district
made more and more progress, so the need for additional sources of water became more urgent. Before the
year 1848 water was supplied to the borough by two
rival companies. The water was obtained from wells,
situated in Bootle and in Toxteth Park. In 1848 the
Town Council bought out the two companies and soon
found that these sources of water were insufficient for
the needs of a rapidly expanding community with a
population of more than 300,000. It was necessary to
look further afield. The Rivington Scheme was begun

in 1852 and finished in 1857. The completion of this
scheme was an important advance in the sanitary
development of the borough and the water supplies
procured from Rivington sufficed for the needs of
Liverpool until 1892 when the Vyrnwy Reservoir was
opened.

The labour and expenditure which were devoted to
the improvement of the sanitary conditions of the
borough of Liverpool from 1847 onwards earned rich
dividends in the improved health of the community.
Writing in the annual report for 1860 Duncan gave
some estimates, based on the Registrar-General's
figures, of the number of lives saved each year as a
result of these sanitary improvements and he summed
up the gains in these terms:

> Looking at these results, and remembering that
> before the passing of the Sanitary Act the annual
> mortality of Liverpool was notoriously and invari-
> ably higher than that of any other town in the king-
> dom, the authorities and ratepayers may congratulate
> themselves that the expenditure for sanitary pur-
> poses since 1847—large as it has been—has borne
> abundant fruit, and that the results have been com-
> mensurate with the sacrifices which have been made.
> It may be hoped that the disparaging remarks
> which have been made from time to time, as to the
> results of sanitary operations in Liverpool, may
> henceforward cease, and that even the most un-
> reasonable may be satisfied that the proceedings of
> the Health Committee have been productive of
> benefit.

The foundation of a sanitary environment in Liverpool was laid by Duncan and Newlands; it was for
their successors to build on it.

9

DUNCAN'S OFFICIAL CORRESPONDENCE

IN writing an appreciation of Duncan's work in Liverpool the author is fortunate in finding in the Public
Health Department offices three letter-books in which
all his correspondence over a period of nearly fourteen
years, written in his own handwriting, is copied. These
books cover the periods during Duncan's tenure of
office from the 16th May, 1849, to the 26th March,
1853; the 4th May, 1853, to the 16th July, 1859; and
the 26th July, 1859, to the 20th April, 1863. Copies of
correspondence from the date of his appointment at the
beginning of 1847 until May, 1849, are missing.
    The letter-books cover the whole of Duncan's period
of office, except the first two years, and during that time
all the office correspondence of an important character
was conducted by the Medical Officer of Health per-
sonally. For some years after his appointment he had
no clerical assistance except in periods of emergency
such as a cholera epidemic, and even when he had the
services of a clerk all letters except routine ones and
all reports to the General Board of Health and to Committees of the Town Council were written in his own
flowing and legible handwriting. Nevertheless, the
volume of official correspondence is relatively small.
The three letter-books, covering Duncan's correspondence during a period of fourteen years, contain about
1,000 letters and reports. Many consist of the small
change of official life—letters to the Spanish and
Portuguese Consuls about the prevalence and non-
prevalence of cholera in the borough, to some individual
concerning the condition of a lodging-house or the

111

existence of a nuisance, to another medical officer regarding mortality statistics, and so on. But a considerable number of letters are of great interest to the student of social, and especially sanitary, conditions in a great seaport during the middle years of last century at a time when Liverpool was a recognized leader in the sphere of sanitary reform.

A perusal of these letters shows that Duncan possessed a clear and logical mind and had the ability to express and explain his views and opinions briefly and precisely. He shows in his correspondence all the old-fashioned courtesy which one had been led to expect of the Victorians but he could, on occasion, display contempt or indignation in forthright terms. There is, however, very little sign of emotion in his official letters; they are always precise, dignified and formal. Seldom does he depart from the formal "My dear Sir," or "Dear Sir" even when writing to people he knows very well. Even Edwin Chadwick of the General Board of Health, whose help he sometimes solicits in time of difficulty and who was an old friend and colleague, he invariably addresses as "My dear Sir." Duncan appears to have had a keen sense of humour which in his official correspondence, as was proper, he kept under strict control. But now and then—all too infrequently—it peeps out. On one occasion an Inspector of the General Board of Health gave him very short notice of an intended visit, unfortunately at a time when Duncan was due to attend a meeting of the Medical Relief Committee—a body of which he held no high opinion. His reply to the Inspector was that he might well visit Liverpool at the time stated and inspect the Medical Relief Committee! There are few letters from Duncan to the heads of the other Corporation Departments, for most of the business between them was settled by personal visits. On one occasion, however, in the early years when the Medical Officer of Health possessed no staff, the Paid Officers' Committee of the Council (see page 53) asked the Town Clerk to circularize the

SIR EDWIN CHADWICK, K.C.B.

various departments and obtain a nominal roll of the officials employed. Duncan's reply was characteristic:

The following list comprises the whole of the officer in my department paid by the Corporation:
William Henry Duncan, M.D.,
Medical Officer of Health.

Humour was, as I have said, exceptional and the conditions under which he was working and the appallingly serious problems with which he was faced did not conduce to frequent levity. Throughout the correspondence Duncan was labouring under one particular overwhelming anxiety—the possibility of a return of the epidemics of cholera. As Physician to the South Dispensary he had faced one epidemic in 1832. After his appointment as Medical Officer of Health in 1847 he had the responsibility of dealing with any outbreaks of this formidable disease, not as a clinician but as an administrator charged with the duty of using or co-ordinating all the borough's available resources to combat the epidemic. This was a difficult task for a single medical officer without departmental resources, and dependent on the co-operation of the Select Vestry which did not always see eye to eye with him either in regard to preliminary arrangements when an outbreak seemed to be threatening or to the measures necessary for dealing with the disease when it had actually appeared in epidemic form. No doubt the Select Vestry had difficulties of its own which were not very clearly apparent to Duncan. It might be criticized both by the General Board of Health and by its constituents in Liverpool if it spent public money in providing for an epidemic which did not occur or, during an outbreak, in opening a hospital which events might show was not required. It was a question of judgment, of coming to conclusions on the basis of very scanty facts, and opinions might reasonably differ as to the proper course to be pursued. In the 1849 epidemic of cholera Duncan was often at loggerheads with the

H

Select Vestry and even later in his career was often critical and suspicious of that body. On the whole the policy of the General Board of Health was to support the Medical Officer rather than the Select Vestry when any question in regard to the control of epidemics arose, and this attitude was especially shown when the Vestry raised the fundamental question of Duncan's powers and duties as laid down in Section 122 of the Liverpool Sanitary Act. The words in the section dealing with the duties of the Medical Officer of Health referred to a legally qualified medical practitioner, of skill and experience,

> To inspect and report periodically on the sanitary condition of the said borough, to ascertain the existence of diseases, more especially epidemics increasing the rates of mortality, and to point out the existence of any nuisances or other local causes which are likely to originate and maintain such diseases and injuriously affect the health of the inhabitants of the said borough, and to take cognisance of the fact of the existence of any contagious disease, and to point out the most efficacious modes for checking or preventing the spread of such diseases. . . .

The argument of the Select Vestry was to the effect that under the section it was the Medical Officer of Health's duty to "inspect and report," "to ascertain the existence of disease," etc., but, having inspected, reported and ascertained, his functions were completed and such action as might be necessary then fell within the scope of the duties of the Vestry which possessed or could obtain the necessary resources in the way of hospitals, parish medical officers or lay or medical visitors. If the General Board of Health had upheld this restricted view of the duties of the Medical Officer of Health there would have been little future for Duncan and his successors; but, fortunately, the Board's opinion favoured the widest extension of the duties of the Medical Officer of Health and as a consequence

Duncan came to be regarded, both by the Board and the Town Council, as the administrator charged, in time of epidemics, with the duty of co-ordinating all the resources of the borough, whether in the possession of the Council or not.

There is little doubt that Duncan's friendly relationship to Chadwick, who was from 1848 to 1854 a Commissioner of the General Board of Health, was of material assistance to him in his fight to extend the duties of a Medical Officer of Health as laid down in the Act of 1846. Duncan occasionally reported direct to Chadwick and sometimes asked his advice. Evidently in 1853 his relations with the Select Vestry were improving, for at the end of a report to Chadwick he said, "The Parish Authorities seem more disposed to do what is required than they were in 1849." One of his personal letters to Mr. Chadwick complained of a mistake made by the General Board of Health in calculating Liverpool's mortality rate:

I have written by to-night's post to your secretary with reference to a serious error pervading his last three letters to me with reference to the rate of mortality in Liverpool. It has since occurred to me that in making the calculation, the population of the parish has been taken in place of that of the borough of Liverpool. The population of the parish is about two-thirds only of that of the borough and on this supposition the error would be accounted for.[1]

I some time ago requested Mr. Newlands to give me a list of the streets, etc. which he mentioned to you as having been remarkably improved by sanitary operations, together with the dates, etc. He has not yet done so but when he does I shall endeavour to ascertain the results and let you know.

There are two more letters to Mr. Chadwick in the first of the three letter-books. One of these, dated the

[1] In 1835, Everton, Kirkdale and the populous parts of West Derby and Toxteth were added to the original Parish of Liverpool; the whole forming the Borough of Liverpool.

28th October, 1851, was in reply to a letter from
Chadwick on the subject of lodging-houses:

> Having been absent from town I did not receive
> your note in time to answer it by yesterday's post.
>
> We have no more recent information on the sub-
> ject of lodging-houses of such a kind as would be
> useful for your present object. I have made one or
> two pencil observations on the Draft, which I return
> herewith.
>
> The hint with regard to the *ab extra* impetus is
> good, as it was that no doubt which led to legislation
> with regard to our cellars. But it might have been
> added that forty years previously their injurious
> effect on health had been pointed out to the Town
> Council by the Physicians of the Infirmary and
> Dispensary in a report drawn up by Dr. Currie.
>
> I send you a copy of my Report which was this
> morning only received from the printer. In a day or
> two I will forward more. The information with
> regard to cellar dwellings in page 98, etc., is some-
> what more recent than you have previously had.

The report referred to is the Medical Officer of
Health's Report for the years 1847–50 towards the end
of which is a full account of the action being taken in
Liverpool to reduce the number of occupied cellars
(see page 77).

The other letter, dated the 16th July, 1852, was a
brief note which forwarded a list of the names of gentlemen here and in the neighbourhood, "some of whom I
know, and others I am *told* take an interest in the
sewage manure question."[1]

His statistical information on the health of Liverpool
was, in one or two cases, addressed to Mr. William
Farr, the medical statistician to the General Register
Office, who first joined that department as a compiler

[1] The Borough Engineer, in his report published in 1851, discusses
at some length the problems involved in obtaining manure from sewage,
and refers to the methods successfully adopted by Mr. Moffat in London.

of abstracts in 1839. One letter to Farr, dated the 13th November, 1849, is as follows:

I am very sorry that my absence from indisposition, had prevented an earlier reply to your note of the 25th ultimo. I make a weekly report to the Health Committee, the report comprising not only a statement as to the health of the town, but also any recommendations I may have to make as to sewering or other sanatory measures; but these reports being made from week to week none of them are printed. I have also made special reports from time to time, but with the exception of a short report in anticipation of the cholera visitation, none of these have been printed, excepting in the local newspapers.

If you will point out the particular kind of information you wish for, it will give me much pleasure to furnish it if in my power, or to make myself useful to you in any way you may mention.

Cholera has, at length, left us, after having existed as an epidemic nearly five months and caused a greater mortality than I had anticipated considering the improved sanatory condition of the town within the last few years. I am inclined to think that cholera is more dependent on influences beyond our control than typhoid fever is; that the "atmospheric constitution" is an element of more power in the former epidemic, and that it has been lost sight of by the Board of Health when they talk of extinguishing the epidemic. I am persuaded that no house-to-house visitation could shorten the duration of the epidemic by a single day, however much it might circumscribe its ravages.

About 10,000 of the worst houses in Liverpool were daily visited, but cholera carried off 5,000 of our people.

Duncan's most interesting letter to Farr was in response to the latter's suggestion that he should examine the question of the influence of elevation on the incidence of cholera in Liverpool. In his letter, dated the 15th May, 1852, reporting the results of his observations, Duncan wrote:

The borough is divided into sixteen municipal wards or districts. In the eight highest districts—having an average elevation of about 100 feet above high-water mark—the mortality from cholera was 90 in 10,000 inhabitants. In the eight lowest districts, with an average elevation of about 35 feet, the mortality was 214 per 10,000. The higher districts had a population of about 186,000; the lower about 165,000.

Dividing the districts into three groups, having as nearly as the arrangement admits of, equal amounts of population, the mortality in the highest group was 59 in 10,000; in the middle group 176 in 10,000; and in the lowest, 211 in 10,000. The average elevation of these groups was respectively about 125, 50, and 30 feet. In the first group the elevations varied from 110 to 160 feet, in the second from 44 to 74 feet, in the third, from 20 to 38 feet.

Taking the districts singly where the difference of elevation is only 2 or 3 feet, I find that the Law is not carried out—being apparently overpowered by disturbing elements which come into operation. But when the districts of approximating elevations are grouped together, and the groups so formed contrasted, the results distinctly point to a relation between the elevation of the soil and the mortality from cholera.

I myself estimated the elevations from the contour map of the borough, so that they cannot be depended on as *strictly* accurate. They are as nearly so, however, as I could make them.[1]

In a further letter to Farr, dated the 3rd June, Duncan referred to the information supplied in his previous letter, saying:

[1] The information contained in this letter gave some support to Farr's theory that "mortality from cholera is in the inverse ratio of the elevation."

You are quite at liberty to make any use you think proper of my letters on cholera. I beg that you will at all times command my services in any way in which you may think them likely to be useful.

In a letter written in July, 1850, to his friend Dr. Sutherland, whom he addresses in a more cordial fashion than any other correspondent, Duncan mentioned that he had had a narrow escape from a Coroner's inquest in consequence of his horse falling back on him; and in another, in February, 1851 (one of his infrequent communications, by letter, to the head of another Corporation Department), he complained to Mr. W. Shuttleworth, the Town Clerk, that in the space of six months he had paid out of his own pocket upwards of twenty pounds for assistance at the office, and had employed his own servant as a messenger, neither clerk nor messenger being allowed by the Committee. "It is not my intention, however," he said, "to continue this arrangement." Duncan used his own gig, horse and groom also on Corporation business, during a period of two and a half years, at an estimated cost to himself of £95 per annum. This seems rather hard on Duncan and is an indication that, even as late as 1851, the Health Committee was not quite used to possessing a Medical Officer of Health and had not fully faced all the implications of the appointment. These were but the teething troubles of a new office; and in the next few years the Health Committee allowed him a clerical staff and five lodging-house inspectors.

Duncan was at all times willing to break a lance in the defence of his native town. Early in 1857 there was a letter to the Editor of *Public Health* protesting about a statement in that journal to the effect that six deaths from destitution had occurred in Liverpool during a week in the previous year. The statement contained an observation that the writer "cannot understand how this can occur in Liverpool where the parochial matters are so regularly arranged." The Medical Officer of

Health wrote severely about the inaccuracies which he had observed from time to time in the reports contained in the journal on the mortality in Liverpool and went on to say categorically that the statement was erroneous, no such deaths having occurred.

Much of Duncan's correspondence was taken up with local matters and the bulk of it dealt with complaints about nuisances, lodging-houses and routine matters of a similar kind. He was just as reluctant to prosecute and just as anxious to offer constructive suggestions to the owners of factories emitting excessive amounts of smoke as a Medical Officer of Health at the present day. In December, 1853, he wrote to a medical correspondent in Manchester to ask for information about the possibility of preventing the nuisance arising from the re-burning of animal charcoal for sugar-refining purposes. Apparently there had been some difficulty of this kind in regard to Messrs. Macfie's, a firm of sugar refiners which, he thought, would not grudge any reasonable expenditure which gave a fair prospect of allowing them to continue the process.

Some nuisances were evidently irremediable and the Health Committee's policy, in the event of a serious nuisance, was to bring pressure to bear upon the owner of the offending factory or works to discontinue the process if no method of mitigating the nuisance could be discovered. Thus, in one letter, he noted that his correspondent had agreed to discontinue the drying of wheat in a kiln at Tempest Hey, about which complaints had been received from residents in that district. Dye-houses appear to have caused some difficulties at that time and Duncan occasionally presented a certificate to the Health Committee condemning a particular process as a nuisance. One is as follows:

> I certify that I have inspected the premises occupied as a Dye-house by Messrs. —— in Ranelagh Street and that the process employed in preparing the colouring matter causes a nuisance injurious to the health of the inhabitants of the adjoining houses.

In the correspondence there is an occasional reference to the dangers attendant upon travel by sea during the middle of the nineteenth century. Thus, in an official report, he made the following observations on this point:

> I beg to report . . . that the ship *Guiding Star* which sailed from this port on the 27th October with about 500 emigrants and put into Belfast Lough on the 5th November with loss of spars and sails, arrived in the river last night, having lost 23 of her passengers from cholera between the 30th October and the 9th November. The whole of the remainder with one exception, were healthy and seemed to have suffered little from the privations to which they had been exposed.

The majority of the passengers on the *Guiding Star* were Irish and German emigrants to the United States. This was one of the periods of extensive emigration from Europe to the New World and the presence of emigrants on ships putting into the Port of Liverpool is occasionally, but only incidentally, mentioned in the correspondence, usually in connection with outbreaks of cholera. It is evident, however, that European emigrants to America a hundred years ago had to suffer the ordeals of the sea in small, ill-found ships, and incurred, in addition, dangers from the more serious of the infectious diseases of which cholera was the most deadly and the most dreaded. These emigrants were the ancestors—German and Irish—of many of the 140 millions in the United States to-day.

There is another report which describes the danger of infection to which passengers, especially in the steerage, were exposed when travelling in the small and crowded ships of those days. Duncan in this report referred to an outbreak of cholera which occurred in August, 1852, on the packet ship *Garrick* sailing from New York to Liverpool. There were about 100 passengers, nearly all steerage. The voyage lasted for twenty-seven days and during that time fourteen of the passengers and crew became ill with cholera and of these thirteen died. It is interesting to note the various explanations of the origins of this outbreak. The passengers ascribed it to the crowded state of the steerage; the ship's doctor and the captain to the fact that many of the steerage passengers insisted on sleeping on deck while the weather was damp and foggy; while Duncan himself thought it probable that the ship had passed through a stratum of atmosphere charged with the cholera poison.

It seems rather surprising, taking into account the crowded state of the steerage accommodation in this vessel, that only fourteen out of more than 100 people contracted cholera—if, indeed, the disease was cholera. Duncan was convinced that it was, and gives the symptoms as purging, vomiting and cramp. The ship's doctor, on the other hand, was certain that the disease was not cholera; but it is difficult to imagine any other disease with these symptoms, terminating fatally in nearly all the cases after a few days' illness.

Some of the correspondence refers to the sewerage schemes which were then being pressed on with all possible speed by the Borough Engineer. Duncan from time to time made specific recommendations to the Health Committee in regard to the sewerage and drainage of particular localities. Sometimes it proved impracticable to sewer and drain certain streets in the poorer quarters of the borough until a main sewer to serve the district had been constructed. The kind of situation referred to in the following letter frequently occurred:

Poplar Street is one of those unfortunate streets for which nothing can be done at present, sewerage being impossible on that side of the slope until the outlet sewer from Kirkdale reaches the locality. Mr. Newlands says this will be in about eight months, but I must say I don't believe him.

Often, however, it was possible to do something about draining some obscure street:

It appears that the sewer in Back Hughes Street is deep enough to drain the middens adjoining St. Mark's School. Notice has accordingly been served on the owners to do so, and also to repair the walls of the ashpit.

There is a reference to quarantine in a letter dated the 22nd October, 1853, and a hint of Duncan's ever-present preoccupation with the possibility of an outbreak of cholera:

On my return home a short time ago after an absence of some weeks on the Continent I found your letter . . . with a copy of your paper on quarantine for which I must return my best thanks. In your views on this subject I think I entirely concur.

With regard to the *Clare Wheeler* I have not been able to ascertain anything beyond the fact that she was not put into quarantine. The Quarantine Office, in fact, knows nothing of her. Should you wish it I shall make further inquiries of the consignees of the ship which, indeed, I should have done before writing to you had I not been too much occupied since my return in making arrangements for the possible outbreak of cholera.

During Duncan's period of office, nightly as well as daily inspections of the large number of lodging-houses which were registered in the borough were undertaken by the inspectors on his staff. In the last of the three letter-books there are several letters to Mr. Theodore W. Rathbone[1] who appears to have criticized the methods of registration and inspection of lodging-

[1] The Rathbone family have for more than a century been notable for public work in Liverpool. Perhaps the most famous member of the family was the late Miss Eleanor Rathbone, Member of Parliament for the Combined English Universities, who was a member of the Liverpool City Council for many years, and who became well known for her advocacy of family allowances. Her father, William Rathbone, was a first cousin of Theodore Rathbone.

houses adopted by the Committee, but this correspondence was conducted without acrimony on both sides and Duncan informed Mr. Rathbone, in one of his letters, that he had never supposed, even when it was suggested to him, that there was anything personal in the criticisms. "I have known both yourself, and Mr. Earle too, long enough," he said, "to feel assured that you can be actuated by no other than the best motives in anything you do."

In a letter to a correspondent in January, 1860, Duncan estimated the population of Liverpool at that time as 458,000, and the rate of yearly increase as about 10,000 during the previous two or three years; and in response to another inquiry he gave the population of the borough in the middle of 1846 as 329,000, and the mid-year population in 1859 as 454,000.

Early in 1860 he was evidently considering the question of the amount of accommodation which his department would require in the new offices (the present Municipal Buildings in Dale Street, opened in 1867) about to be constructed by the Town Council. In a letter to the Borough Engineer, Mr. Newlands, he described the proposed accommodation as well adapted to his purposes, adding the hope that it would be so situated as to be easily found by very stupid people, "a number of whom call on me daily."

In another letter, written in the same year, Duncan displayed for the first time in his official correspondence some interest in the design of dwellings for the working classes, for he expressed the opinion that the great desideratum should be cheapness and an efficient mode of ventilation. He also mentioned Liverpool's baths and wash-houses and the lead the borough took in the matter.

Writing to Dr. Sutherland,[1] of the General Board of

[1] Dr. John Sutherland (1808–91) graduated M.D. at Edinburgh University in 1831. He practised for a short period in Liverpool where he edited the *Liverpool Health of Towns' Advocate* in 1846. He became an inspector of the General Board of Health in 1848 and during the Crimean War became head of a commission sent to the Crimea to inquire

Health, in April, 1861, Dr. Duncan referred to a few cases of typhus which had occurred at the Southern Hospital, and said, "So far it almost seems a case of generation of fever from animal filth and effluvia, but the escape of the men themselves is the anomaly in the case."

A letter to Dr. W. T. Gairdner, of Edinburgh, written in June, 1861, gave Duncan the opportunity of making a short survey of sanitary progress in Liverpool since his appointment:

In reply to your first question I may state that every house in Liverpool has a supply of water with the exception of court houses, many of which also have an independent supply, but with regard to which the rule is that a single tap in each court supplies all the houses in that court. You are probably aware that a few years ago the Town Council brought a new supply from a distance of more than thirty miles at a cost of about £1,500,000. This, with three of the most productive wells formerly in use and still retained, yields about 14 millions gallons daily—about 30 gallons a head for every man, woman and child. It suffices for watering the streets, flushing the sewers, washing the courts, etc., and supplying a large number of drinking fountains in the more densely peopled districts of the town.

With regard to drainage, I am unable in the absence of the Borough Engineer to give you the precise figures but I believe I am near the truth in saying that since our Sanitary Act came into operation in 1847 about 180 miles of main sewers have been constructed and more than 40,000 houses have been drained into those sewers, in addition to which nearly

---

into the sanitary condition of the English troops. There he came into touch with Florence Nightingale and shares with her the credit for the improvement in the provision for the sick and wounded. Sutherland was appointed medical superintending inspector-general of the Board of Health and Home Office in 1888.

every court in Liverpool has been drained—representing at least 12,000 houses more.

The inhabited houses at the late Census were 66,000, and I estimate that the number of houses remaining undrained does not exceed one-fourth of the whole. The work is still going on at the rate of about 2,000 yearly in excess of the number of new houses erected.

In a postscript to this letter he added:

When I first called attention to the subject, I believe that not a single court in Liverpool was drained. Very few instead are now undrained.

During each year the Medical Officer of Health received many inquiries about the administration of his department, especially on the subject of the staff required to perform various duties. The following is the reply to one of these inquiries. It was dated the 24th July, 1861, and was addressed to the Chief Constable of Newcastle-upon-Tyne:

In reply to your note (handed to me by Major Greig) inquiring as to the number of lodging-house inspectors, I beg to say they consist of:

(1) One Chief Inspector and four Inspectors.

(2) They are on duty eight hours daily, excepting on alternate days when they are only five hours on duty during the day, having been two and a half hours on duty during the previous night (from 11.30 to 2).

(3) The town is divided into four districts for the purpose of the inspection, each officer having on an average rather more than 200 registered lodging-houses in his district.

(4) The Chief Inspector receives 33s. and each of the four Inspectors 30s. per week and uniform.

These officers, although formerly members of the Police Force, are now quite unconnected with it.

Major Greig was the Head Constable of Liverpool at that time. Although the senior police officer in most towns and counties was called "Chief" Constable, this practice was not adopted in Liverpool until 1920. The lodging-house inspectors were on the staff of the Medical Officer of Health and were recruited from the police. There are several letters in the correspondence referring to interviews by the Health Committee of a list of police officers recommended by Major Greig as being likely candidates for the post of lodging-house inspector.

The number of lodging-houses in Liverpool was at that time very large, but not remarkably so when the nature of the town, as a great port, is taken into consideration. At some periods the number registered was over 1,000 but in many instances their life was very short, some being on the register for a few months only. Thus, in the monthly report to the Health Committee dated the 15th December, 1862, it is mentioned that there were 1,007 lodging-houses on the register and that 56 had been given up during the past eight weeks. In one of his letters Duncan instituted a comparison, on a population basis, between the number of lodging-houses in Liverpool and some of the other large towns, Liverpool being at the head of the list.

Writing to the Medical Officer of Health of Barnsley, late in 1861, he gave some interesting information on the subject of the opposition experienced in connection with the Rivington Scheme:

I have never heard any objection to the Rivington water on the ground of its softness although there is no doubt that the hard water from the sandstone is preferable for *drinking* to the soft catchment water. For every other purpose the soft water is to be preferred and as I have said I have heard of no objection, even for drinking, to the Rivington water as being too soft, but there is a general objection to it on account of the brownish tinge which it acquires from the peaty bottom of a large portion of the gathering ground. We talk of improving our filtering arrangements in the hope of getting rid of at least some portion of the remaining colour.

The mean of four analyses of the Rivington water . . . gives about 2 degrees of hardness, but our supply is partly obtained from wells in the sandstone—not for the purpose of diluting the Rivington water or improving its colour but simply because the quantity yet received from Rivington is insufficient for our requirements. The town was formerly supplied by seven wells; four of these have been given up, the three most productive are still pumped. The mean hardness of these is about 12 degrees.

The quantity of water supplied to the town for the last few weeks has averaged 103,000,000 gallons weekly, one part well water to three parts Rivington.

The cost of the Rivington works has largely exceeded the estimate—partly, it is alleged by the advocates of the scheme (I believe with truth) on account of the pertinacious opposition which it encountered, but also from the necessity of acquiring additional gathering ground to satisfy the unexpectedly large requirements of the mill-owners, etc., whose supplies of water were cut off by our operations, and who were consequently entitled to "compensation" water.

In a letter to a member of the Registrar-General's staff Duncan referred to the controversy arising out of a comparison between the mortality returns of Liverpool and Ely contained in one of the Quarterly Reports (see page 102). After discussing deaths from various diseases in Liverpool he continued:

The excess of violent deaths is no doubt connected with the shipping to a great extent, but London has shipping also. If you will consent to compare the mortality of "Liverpool" with that of the East End of London, I will make no objection; but in the gloomy pictures which you sanitary censors take such delight in drawing of the town to whose example you all owe so much, I have no recollection that you are in the habit of comparing Liverpool with districts of analogous character. That would be obviously unfair! A little pleasingly situated country town, or big village like Ely answers the purpose much better!

Writing in response to an inquiry from the Officer of Health of Newport, Duncan discussed the use for human food of animals smothered on the voyage between Spain or Ireland and this country. He would not necessarily declare such animals unfit for human consumption, much depending on the duration of the voyage and the extent of the injuries and particularly as to whether the animal lived long enough to allow of fever being developed; but he mentioned that in Liverpool there was a local Act under which *all* smothered cattle arriving at the port were seized and boiled down for the benefit of the owners. He informed his correspondent that the Medical Officer of Health did not necessarily see meat before condemnation, this duty being performed by the four Inspectors of Slaughter-houses employed by the Corporation.

From time to time Duncan, like other house-holders with less sanitary knowledge, had sanitary difficulties at his own home and his reactions in such circumstances did not differ very much from those of his neighbours. Thus, to a correspondent, in September, 1862:

I regret much that I cannot give a satisfactory reply to your note, being a fellow sufferer from the same cause, and my landlord's efforts to afford a remedy having hitherto failed. By poisoning their tracks and plastering the holes by which they made their entrance from the adjoining house some months ago, I hoped they had been induced to pass on to my next neighbour, but on my return to town on Saturday I was informed that they had reappeared and this morning their pickets or advance guard were dis-

covered for the first time in the library—the room
over the kitchen to which the invasion had previously
been confined. When they have once fairly taken
possession of a house I fear there is nothing for it but
inglorious flight and leaving the field in possession
of the enemy.

There is an engaging mixture of humour and resig-
nation in this letter which throws an interesting side-
light on Duncan's character. If rats could be such a
plague in the better-class houses it is not difficult to
conceive of the harm they must have caused in the
lower quarters of the borough. There is scanty mention
of these pests in the literature of the time—they are
never even referred to in the Medical Officer of Health's
reports—and it must be supposed they were regarded, as
Duncan appears to have regarded them, as one of the inevitable trials of life to be borne with Christian fortitude.

In this letter-book there is part of a letter in Duncan's
handwriting (written in 1863) which deals with the
average age at death of the Liverpool population. The
addressee's name is not copied. The information given
is that the average age at death of all who died (7,613
persons) in the Parish of Liverpool in the year 1860
was $25\frac{1}{2}$ years (25 years 5 months 23 days). Duncan
commented that in Dr. Lyon Playfair's report on the
large towns in Lancashire (see page 37) it was stated
that the average age of death in Liverpool in the years
1841–2 was 20 years, which showed an improvement
of five years and a half in the interval of nineteen years.
These figures, it will be noted, refer to the Parish—the
average age at death in the Borough, which contained
some of the less thickly populated districts, would
undoubtedly be higher. As an indication of the progress
made since that time it is interesting to compare the
figure of $25\frac{1}{2}$ years as the average age at death in the
Liverpool of 1860 with that of the modern city, viz.
55 years in 1944.

One of the remarkable things about this official correspondence is the fact that the Medical Officer of Health, in spite of the position of Liverpool as a great port and as a leader in sanitary reform, had little direct contact with the Continent or the United States. The only letter written by him to a correspondent in the United States during his period of office and copied in the letter-books is one addressed to Mr. Lemuel Shattuck, the great sanitary reformer, of Boston, Mass., in December, 1849. This letter is too long to be given in full; but it discussed the sanitary progress made in Liverpool during the period since the Sanitary Act was passed and referred to his hope of future progress. Accompanying the letter were a large number of reports on health conditions in Liverpool and other parts of this country, copies or abstracts of Liverpool and general legislation on sanitary matters and of by-laws relating to lodging-houses, etc. Duncan also described the working of the system of baths and wash-houses in Liverpool and said that six more were about to be constructed—so great had been the success of the previous ones. He referred to the tenements for the labouring classes erected in Birkenhead and expressed the opinion that on sanitary grounds these dwellings could not be recommended as models for imitation.

Although several years have elapsed since their erection [he added] they have been and still are, unoccupied—in consequence, perhaps, of the deserted condition of Birkenhead.

Since our local Act came into operation the sanatory condition of Liverpool has been wonderfully improved. The drainage and cleansing of the worst districts, the enforced cleansing of the dwellings of the poor, the flagging of the courts and passages, etc., have effected wonders. The mortality of Liverpool is at present lower than I have ever previously known it.

I congratulate you on the active part which the reports forwarded to me show that you have taken in the Sanatory Cause. . . .

Duncan's statement about the low mortality in Liverpool at that time seems inexplicable in the light of the fact that the borough had just passed through one of the worst epidemics in its history. This letter, however, makes interesting reading. Between the lines of the polite and formal phrasing one can discern the burning zeal and enthusiasm of the reformer, and can sense the spirit of the man who had given up freedom and independence and the financial rewards of a successful medical practice in order to undertake the heartbreaking and thankless task of improving the healthfulness of the poorer quarters of his native borough.

During this fourteen years' correspondence there were times when the incidence of infectious diseases was at its minimum, and in quiet periods of this kind Duncan's letters were almost wholly concerned with simple matters of sanitation. It was then no doubt that the main advances in this direction were made. Many of his monthly reports to the Council's Health Committee were at such times concerned with the inspection of lodging-houses, in which, as Medical Officer of Health, he took a very special interest as potential breeding grounds of epidemic diseases.

Occasionally there is a letter to a practitioner, such as the following, which is by no means unlike those written by a modern Medical Officer of Health:

In reference to the case of Mary —— whom you lately attended in her confinement, I understand you to wish my opinion as to whether there was anything in the length of your attendance which should give rise to the suspicion that the case was not one of puerperal fever.

Having seen the notes of your visits to the patient in question, I unhesitatingly answer in the negative, and can only express my belief that there has been a mistake in supposing any medical man to have stated "real puerperal fever would require a much more lengthened attendance."

As far as I can judge, the case comes within the intention of Art. 182 of the General Order of the Poor Law Board, of the 8th December, 1847.

Let me add that no one who knows your character for integrity and honour could for a moment suppose you capable of making a claim to which you did not conscientiously believe yourself to be justly entitled.

In a letter to a clergyman early in 1851, he gave the following table of deaths registered in the Borough of Liverpool:

TABLE VI

Years	All Causes	Zymotic Diseases	Consumption
1848	12,211	4,348	1,361
1849	17,047	8,559	1,357
1850	10,123	2,649	1,265
Average	13,127	5,185	1,328

In this table the calamitous year of 1849 stands out. Indeed, these few figures by themselves clearly indicate the instability of the health situation of the industrial towns in England in the middle of last century, when such violent fluctuations could take place in the number of deaths from zymotic diseases. Apart from deaths from these diseases the three years for which figures are given show remarkably little difference in the number of deaths from consumption and causes other than zymotic diseases.

An interesting report refers to methods of boiling down the carcases of smothered cattle (see page 129). Apparently one method tried was to use various strengths of hydrochloric acid, partly to reduce the time spent in the process and partly to mitigate the nuisance inseparable from the method of disposing of the carcases:

The Medical Officer of Health, having inspected the process of boiling down the carcases of smothered cattle with the aid of acids, and having examined the

proposed site of the depot in St. Andrew Street, begs
to report as follows:

With regard to the alleged effect of the acids to
expedite the process and so diminish the duration of
the nuisance—in the limited experiments witnessed
they had this effect, but in no material degree. Were
a larger proportion of acids employed the process
would, no doubt, be completed in a shorter time, but
of course at an increased expense. In an equal time
the fatty matter appeared to be more completely
extracted by the acidulated liquor than by the water
without the addition of acid; and it is stated that the
acid had the effect of giving a proper consistence to
the fat—an effect not easily attained without it.

As regards the power of the acids to destroy the
noxious effluvia—in the experiments referred to the
smell was sensibly diminished but by no means
destroyed. It still remained offensive but mixed with
the smell of chlorine gas evolved by the decompo-
sition of the hydrochloric acid.

The noxious smell would probably be more considerably diminished by passing the steam through
the furnace, but as the Medical Officer of Health has
had no practical experience of the effect of this
process, he is unable to report decidedly as to its
probable success. With regard to the allegation in
the memorial of the inhabitants of Rodney Street
Ward that the acid liquor would have the effect of
loosening the mortar of the sewers, the Medical
Officer of Health is of opinion that there are no sub-
stantial grounds for apprehending danger from this
source. But with reference to the objection to the
proposed site on the ground of its proving a nuisance
to the locality he is of opinion that it is well founded
and that the use of acids—to whatever extent it may
be carried—cannot prevent the process causing a
nuisance injurious to health, if carried on in the pro-
jected site, surrounded as it is by dwelling houses
and in the centre of the town.

The idea of segregating offensive trades in the non-residential parts of the town does not appear to have occurred to the minds of the sanitarians of that day. Indeed, the choice of a site for the process referred to in the foregoing letter, close to the most select residential districts of the Liverpool of 1851, seems a particularly inappropriate one. One expression of opinion in this report is indicative of the speed with which Duncan's mind seized upon the essential fact of any given situation—the suggestion, whether his own idea or not, that the gases produced by the process should be rendered harmless by passing them through the furnace. This idea has of course been used frequently since those days in connection with offensive trades and other processes, and is one of several methods employed to prevent the escape into the atmosphere of noxious fumes from industrial undertakings.

In a communication addressed to the Clerk to the Select Vestry early in 1851, Dr. Duncan referred to the fact, which was causing him some anxiety, that small-pox at that time was on the increase in the borough and that a large proportion of the fatal cases had been unprotected by vaccination. "During the last seven weeks," he informed Mr. Hart, "thirty-four deaths from smallpox have occurred in the parish and of these not less than twenty-one (perhaps more) were unvaccinated. The mortality is now three times the average for the last three years." He suggested that placards should be issued by the Select Vestry (which was the vaccination authority) in an attempt to persuade the "poorer classes" of the need to have their children vaccinated at the proper age. Duncan had some cause for concern about the number of deaths from smallpox in 1851, for they amounted to 354. About two months later he wrote to the Chairman of the Medical Relief Committee of the Select Vestry to say that thirty-five further deaths from smallpox in unvaccinated persons had occurred, and repeated his suggestion about the issue of placards.

Vaccination against smallpox was not then compulsory. Infant vaccination became compulsory as a result of the passage of the Vaccination Act, 1867, and has continued to be nominally compulsory until now.[1] Until 1930 the Vaccination Authority was the Board of Guardians, but the Local Government Act, 1929, which came into force on the 1st April, 1930, transferred this function, amongst others, to the councils of county councils and county boroughs in the provinces and within the area of the County of London to the metropolitan boroughs. The Vaccination Authority for the City of London is the Common Council.

Amongst the letters written about this time was one to Mr. Edward Cardwell, M.P., on the subject of Liverpool's mortality statistics. Cardwell was one of the Liverpool Members of Parliament at that time, but he lost his seat in 1852, and later found another constituency at Oxford. His main interest was in the reform of the Army. He became Secretary of State for War in 1868 and amongst his reforms were the abolition of the purchase of commissions and the institution of the short service system and the reserve. He was raised to the peerage as Viscount Cardwell of Ellerbeck in 1874 and died in 1886.

A long letter to the Officer of Health of Southampton written on the 8th March, 1851, in reply to a number of questions, gives much information about sanitary progress in Liverpool. Duncan mentioned, first of all, the inspection of lodging-houses and gave some details of the incidence of infectious diseases in them, differentiating between registered and unregistered lodging-houses. In the 1849 cholera epidemic there were, it appears, not less than 10,000 cases. The sleeping space for each lodger was 250 cubic feet. At that time there were already a number of public urinals and others were being erected. He mentioned that there had been a trial of a machine for sweeping the streets but that sweeping by hand had been found to be more satisfactory. He

[1] The Vaccination Acts, 1867–1907, are repealed by the National Health Service Act, 1946.

described the water supply in Liverpool as being of good quality but insufficient in quantity; and as regards the sewerage system in the older parts of the borough he considered it good but said that in the out-townships little had been done as the Health Committee had no control of it until 1847. There were at the time of writing two baths and wash-house establishments with a third in the course of erection, and sites for four more had been purchased by the Corporation. Duncan gives the interesting information that during the winter quarter at the two establishments open there were 14,535 bathers (this presumably means attendances) and 26,484 dozen of clothes were washed.

He proceeds:

The mortality of Liverpool last year was about 2·73 per cent. Ten years ago it was on an average of years about 3·33 per cent. . . .

Our present cemeteries are all within the limits of the borough; two of the three, however, in thinly peopled parts of the out-townships. A new Parish Cemetery is nearly ready for opening at Walton, about two miles from the town. . . .

I am unable to answer your question as to the increase of prostitution. . . .

The classifying, localizing and registering unfortunate females, I am inclined to look upon as impracticable in this country. . . .

The question as to whether there would be a pecuniary saving by placing the sanitary condition of a town of 36,000 inhabitants on a right basis, can only be answered in one way. There can be no doubt that there would; that is to say the Poor Rate would be less *ceteris paribus*, in such a town than in one where these matters had not been attended to. . . .

The health of the worst conditioned districts is decidedly improved since our Sanatory Act came into operation.

In March, 1851, he wrote to the Town Clerk on the

subject of the need for a new Emigrants' Home in the borough. He emphasized that it was not so much additional accommodation of this kind which was required as accommodation of a better character, observing that if there were effective supervision of the lodging-houses, the amount of accommodation might be safely left to private enterprise.

The system of man catching might no doubt be materially checked by more stringent regulations and a different organization of the agency offices. . . .

I cannot say that the present licensed lodging-houses are airy and roomy dwellings and furnished with all necessary for the proper reception of emigrants. . . .

My opinion on the whole matter may be thus summed up. I doubt whether an Emigrants' Home would be successful in drawing to it the class of emigrants who most require its protection and who would prefer the comparatively unrestricted freedom of a private lodging-house; but to whatever extent successful, I believe it would be of advantage to the emigrants themselves. It would, of course, to the same extent inflict an injury on the private lodging-house keeper, and on the small tradesmen and shopkeepers in the neighbourhood.

You are perhaps aware that an Emigrants' Home is already in operation, in Moorfields, in what was formerly the British Hotel. I intend to bring it before the Committee on Thursday next for registration. It is calculated for 300 emigrants and I believe that nearly that number of Hungarian refugees are now located there. Another Emigrants' Home is about to be established, under Roman Catholic auspices, in Vulcan Street, near the Clarence Dock.

I trust you will be able, from the above, to judge in how far my evidence would be useful to you or otherwise. The other side have threatened me with a

Speaker's Order; whether it is intended to be carried into effect I do not know.

This correspondence apparently refers to a Bill to be promoted in Parliament by some unspecified society for the purpose of opening an Emigrants' Home, under special safeguards, and it appears that the Town Council were opposing this Bill and had instructed the Town Clerk to petition against it. Subsequent letters show that the solicitors for the promoters of the Bill had taken action to require Duncan's attendance at the hearing and he was requested to deliver to them a summary of his proposed evidence. He replied to the effect that he had no personal objections to this course but that he would have to consult with the Town Clerk as to the propriety of doing so. A day or two later he informed the solicitors that the Town Clerk had obtained the instructions of the Town Council and as a consequence of this he (Duncan) regretted that he was unable to send them an outline of his probable evidence.

Early in 1853 Duncan wrote to the Clerk to the Board of Guardians in Birmingham, informing him of a scheme adopted by the Select Vestry of Liverpool to place their district medical officers on a full-time basis:

The Chairman of your Board of Guardians has been misinformed with regard to the number of District Surgeons in the Parish of Liverpool. There were formerly thirteen, who were all allowed private practice, but the Select Vestry . . . lately resolved to try the experiment of enlarging the districts, reducing the number of surgeons ultimately to six. This process of reduction is now going on gradually, as vacancies occur; but there are still not fewer than eight or nine surgeons.

I see I have omitted to mention a very important part of the new system which is that the medical officers are to be debarred from private practice, giving their whole time to the parish duties. The salary is £200—with vaccination fees.

In a further letter to the same correspondent the information was given that the parish supplied medicine, the district officers' prescriptions being made up at the Parish Dispensaries. This system of dispensing at Parish Dispensaries is partially in force in Liverpool at the present day, but district medical officers are no longer full-time.

Accommodation for prisoners at the Corporation's Bridewells was causing the Head Constable some anxiety at that time and he asked Duncan to inspect them. The report, dated the 31st January, 1853, was highly unfavourable:

The following is the result of my inspection of the four District Bridewells. The point on which I understood you to ask my opinion was as to the sufficiency of the ventilation. My reply is simply that in three of the Bridewells, viz. Jordan Street, Hotham Street and Vauxhall, no special provision is made for ventilation, and in the fourth—Rose Hill—the only ventilation is by openings communicating with a passage into which the drain which carried off the foul water from the cells gives admission frequently to most offensive effluvia. As there is no sewer in the neighbourhood, this drain discharges itself into the soil below the foundation of the building.

But the point which struck me most was the very inadequate accommodation in all the Bridewells, but especially in Vauxhall and Rose Hill for the number of prisoners occasionally confined in them. The Inspectors of Prisons require 1,000 cubic feet for each prisoner in the gaols of this country, but latterly only our minimum standard for common lodging-houses [has been] 250 cubic feet. The following shows the number of prisoners for whom there is adequate accommodation in each Bridewell, and the number sometimes actually lodged there (as on Saturday or Sunday nights, etc.) according to the statement of the Bridewell keepers:

TABLE VII

	Prisoners for whom there is accommodation	Prisoners actually confined occasionally
Jordan Street	7	12
Hotham Street	10	17
Rose Hill	10	22
Vauxhall	9	30
Total	36	81

I do not know that I need add anything to these facts. You will be able to draw your own conclusions.

The last letter to be reproduced from Duncan's correspondence refers, perhaps appropriately, to the incidence of the communicable diseases—his main preoccupation—and to the mortality of the borough. It is as follows:

In the previous year—1846—the deaths in the Parish of Liverpool . . . were 411 in each 10,000 inhabitants. In the following years they were as under, viz.:

TABLE VIII

1847	716 in 10,000
1848	383 ,, ,,
1849	519 ,, ,,
1850	293 ,, ,,
1851	339 ,, ,,
1852	330 ,, ,,

In making a comparison with previous years, 1847 and 1849 ought not, in fairness, to be included, as they were years of the greatest mortality ever experienced, or that probably ever will be experienced, in Liverpool—from the causes referred to in my report. They were in 1847, the year of Irish famine which sent its starving thousands into Liverpool to spread fever through the town, and 1849, the year of epidemic cholera. The Irish Fever extended throughout the first quarter of 1848, thereby raising the aggregate mortality of the year, but still, taking the average of the four years 1848–50–51–52, it gives a mortality of only 336 in 10,000 inhabitants, which is lower than the average of previous years.

The author has carefully read the whole of Duncan's available correspondence and has attempted to select for inclusion in this chapter letters which either have an intrinsic interest or which might give to the reader an impression of the duties performed by the Medical Officer of Health of an industrial town nearly a hundred years ago. Most of the correspondence is of a humdrum and routine character—detailing the day-to-day work of a medical man turned administrator who, by a process of trial and error, was, with his colleagues the Borough Engineer and the Inspector of Nuisances, building the administrative foundations of a sanitary environment. But for their work and the work of others, it might have been impossible for mankind to continue to live in densely populated urban communities. Duncan made a number of mistakes, the most important of which was his expectation that a programme of sanitary reform was likely to produce rapid results in the direction of a reduction in the mortality returns of the borough. It was this expectation which led him to react so violently whenever any person in authority, such as Farr or Greenhow, criticized adversely Liverpool's mortality statistics, and it was for this reason that he repeatedly argued that the death-rates for the years when severe epidemics occurred should be omitted from the general averages over a period of years. He failed to realize, or at least to admit, that his main duty as Medical Officer of Health, as laid down in the Act and interpreted by the Board of Health, was to reduce the incidence of epidemic disease, and that unless the policy which he adopted had this effect there was little justification for his appointment. Fortunately, both for his generation and the generations which followed, the Health Committee's policy of sanitary reform, so ably carried out by Newlands and Duncan, was the only policy which would, in the long run, reduce the incidence of the most severe of the epidemic diseases and would, besides, make the borough, as year by year it increased in size, tolerable to live in. It was never necessary for succeeding generations to scrap any of the work which the sanitary reformers carried out; it was necessary only to expand and enlarge it. Many of the main sewers built in those days are still in [use; water is still obtained from Rivington and the Green Lane wells; and the methods of inspection of common lodging-houses and slaughter-houses employed by Duncan in the middle of last century would be regarded as perfectly satisfactory at the present day.

The great work of cleansing the borough of Liverpool, initiated in 1847, was to take much time. The day was to come when the borough would be efficiently drained and sewered and sufficient water supplies for all purposes made available. But that day was two decades ahead and Duncan was not destined to live to see it; and, in the meantime, the borough had to face the epidemics of 1847, 1849, 1854 and 1866, and the Medical Officers of Health—Duncan for the first three and Trench for the last—would deal with them to the best of their ability.

10

PROGRESS IN PUBLIC HEALTH IN THE LAST HUNDRED YEARS

DURING the last two or three years of his career Duncan appeared to be failing. There are some indications of the feeble state of his health in the correspondence for 1861 and 1862, as somewhat frequently he mentions that he has been away ill when apologizing for a delay in replying to a letter. It may be supposed that his exertions in the epidemics which ravaged the borough during his period of office from 1847 to 1863 had an adverse effect upon his health; but there is no evidence that he ever contracted typhus or cholera in spite of the fact that, in the course of his duties, he repeatedly visited the districts in which these diseases occurred. In this immunity he was more fortunate than some of his professional colleagues who died in the 1847 and 1849 epidemics.

The last official document signed by Dr. Duncan is dated the 20th April, 1863, and, as was perhaps appropriate, was a monthly report to the Health Committee. The two succeeding documents are also reports to the Health Committee, dated the 25th May and the 15th June, and are signed by Dr. Cameron who had for a number of years acted as Duncan's part-time deputy. In the first report Cameron refers to himself as "acting for the Medical Officer of Health" but in the second he adopts the official style of "Acting Medical Officer of Health."

The next document copied in the letter-book is dated the 20th July, 1863, and is signed by Dr. W. S. Trench who had succeeded Duncan as Medical Officer of Health. William Henry Duncan had died at Elgin on the 23rd May, 1863. He was fifty-seven years of age and had been Medical Officer of Health of the Borough of Liverpool for sixteen years.

Duncan was buried in the Forsyth family vault at Elgin Cathedral, and the following are the brief particulars on his tombstone:

WILLIAM HENRY DUNCAN, M.D.
of Liverpool
Son-in-Law of William Duncan MacAndrew of
Liverpool
And Anne Forsyth, his wife
Died at Elgin on the 23rd May, 1863, aged 57
Catherine MacAndrew, Widow of the above
passed away at Richmond, Surrey, on the
7th February, 1909, aged 78
There Remaineth therefore a Rest to the People
of God
Heb. iv. 9.

The death of Dr. Duncan was announced in the *Liverpool Mercury* on the 26th May, 1863, in the following terms:

It is with regret we have to announce the death of Dr. Duncan, Medical Officer for the Borough of Liverpool. The deceased had been for some months in a delicate state of health, though no immediate danger was apprehended. Recently he paid a visit to some relatives at Elgin, in the north of Scotland, where he died suddenly on Saturday afternoon last.

The name of Dr. Duncan was first brought into notice in connection with the sanitary state of towns by a little work which he published on the subject about the year 1843. At a public meeting held in April, 1845, under the presidency of the then Mayor, for the establishment of a Liverpool branch in aid of the Health of Towns Association, Dr. Duncan made a long and interesting speech showing that he had

K

thoroughly mastered the important subject discussed. It was not a matter of surprise, therefore, that on the establishment of a health committee in Liverpool the services of a gentleman who had paid so much attention to the health of the town should be solicited in the capacity of Medical Officer of Health. The Health Committee of that day was a joint committee of gentlemen who had no high appreciation of the duties that should devolve upon such an officer, and in January, 1847, Dr. Duncan was appointed Medical Officer of Health at a salary of £300 with the privilege of attending to private practice. The Home Secretary reproved the committee for fixing so low a salary and after considerable delay and correspondence, the result was that in January, 1848, Dr. Duncan received the appointment from the Council at the salary of £750 per year, it being understood that he was to relinquish private practice and devote his whole time to the duties of his office. Previously to his appointment, Dr. Duncan was connected with the Infirmary and the Dispensaries in the capacity of honorary physician to those institutions.

For some months deceased had been unable to discharge his official duties which have been temporarily performed by Dr. Cameron. Under the provisions of the Sanitary Act the Town Council have power to recommend a successor to the late Dr. Duncan, but subject to the sanction of the Government authorities.

On the same day the *Daily Post* quoted in its columns an extract from the *Albion* of the previous evening:

The deceased gentleman [Dr. Duncan] who was appointed Medical Officer of Health under the Sanatory Act of 1847, has occupied that onerous and important position ever since, and by his untiring zeal and intelligence, added to the skilful exertions of Mr. Newlands, the Borough Engineer, was instrumental in greatly improving the sanitary conditions of the town. During the whole of the occupancy of the position, he was untiring in devotion to his duties, and his quiet, unobtrusive and retiring disposition added with his gentleness of manner and the unaffected kindliness of deportment, endeared him to all who came into contact with him or who enjoyed the privilege of his friendship. Dr. Duncan was the first to draw attention to the sad conditions of the Vauxhall district and his pamphlet on the subject helped to draw public attention to the unhealthy state of our towns. The doctor followed that pamphlet by further statistical returns and when a Medical Officer of Health was wanted, the choice very properly fell upon him.

After quoting the above extract from the *Albion* the *Daily Post* goes on to make its own comments on the situation which had arisen as a result of the sudden death of the Medical Officer of Health:

> Circumstances since then have greatly changed. We have now a sanitary staff and the parish has appointed a large medical staff. Thus Dr. Duncan had nothing to do. The returns made weekly to the Health Committee are furnished by the registrars and paid for by the Council and these returns will, of course, be continued on the same terms. There is, therefore, no longer any occasion for a medical officer at a salary of £700 a year. Under the Act there must be one but not one whose full time would be required. Many practitioners would be glad to undertake the duty at a reasonable remuneration.

Fortunately, the Town Council did not take the view expressed by the *Daily Post*, and shortly after Duncan's death appointed in his place as full-time Medical Officer of Health Dr. William Stewart Trench.

At the weekly meeting of the Health Committee, Mr. Bowring, the Chairman of the Committee, in expressing his regrets at Dr. Duncan's death, said:

K*

It would be in the remembrance of the Committee that it was to Dr. Duncan's active exertions that the town was indebted for the Sanatory Act passed in 1846 which had proved so beneficial to the health of the town in lessening the rate of mortality from 39 in the 1,000 in 1846 to 27 in the 1,000 in the year before last. After the passing of the Act it was considered that Dr. Duncan would be the most fitting person to carry out the operations required under its provisions. He was therefore appointed medical officer of the borough and he had continued to fill that office to the entire satisfaction of the committee and the public generally from that time until his death.

It is not possible, after the lapse of so many years, to gain a very clear impression of William Henry Duncan as a man rather than as an official. Some aspects of his character, however, can be gleaned from a perusal of his pamphlets, reports and correspondence. The formal style of his correspondence is in keeping with the manners and customs of the age in which he lived and affords no indication of his personality and character. Many of his colleagues in other towns wrote to him for advice and he spared no pains to help them. He was indisputably most diligent and conscientious in his work, which he had chosen in preference to a clinical career and which, in spite of its disadvantages at that time, he evidently enjoyed. The bent of his mind was precise and judicial and it is clear that he delighted in framing reports and in drafting rules and regulations. The Liverpool Sanitary Act, 1846, and the Amendment Act of 1854, owed much to Duncan's ideas and experience and—one may suspect—to his skill in draughtsmanship. The various by-laws used in the Public Health Department during his period of office—in particular those relating to lodging-houses and slaughter-houses—were almost certainly, at least in part, the work of the Medical Officer of Health. As a local pioneer in sanitary reform Duncan was inevitably faced with much opposition, often of a minor character, during the years which followed the passing of the Sanitary Act when he had the task of persuading an intensely individualistic population and its representatives on the Town Council to accept sanitary rules and regulations, the object of which many persons failed to understand, in the larger interests of the public weal. In his favour was the fact that Chadwick and the various commissions on the state of the labouring classes had for many years publicized the urgent need of sanitary improvements; and as if to point the moral, serious epidemics of cholera and typhus, occurring year after year in the large towns, had warned the people that immediate action was imperative.

Duncan occasionally corresponded with Dr. John Simon, Medical Officer of Health of the City of London, who in 1855 was appointed Medical Officer of the General Board of Health, and, in 1858, Medical Officer to the Privy Council. Simon, who was knighted in 1887 (K.C.B.), published a series of reports on health conditions throughout England and Wales, but he is perhaps best known as the author of the famous *English Sanitary Institutions*, in the course of which he surveyed health and social conditions in this country from the earliest times. In Chapter XII he referred to the efforts which Liverpool had made to improve the environmental conditions in the borough notably by procuring the passage of Acts of Parliament relating to water supplies, street improvements, public buildings, sewerage and drainage and general sanitation; and to the appointment, under the provisions of Section 122 of the Liverpool Sanitary Act, 1846, of Dr. W. H. Duncan as Medical Officer of Health, "the earliest of the medical profession to hold any such office in this country."

Sir John Simon's appraisal of the work performed by Duncan in Liverpool is well worth quoting:

Dr. Duncan, a native of Liverpool, had long been

known there as a leader of local opinion and action in the movement for sanitary reform. As far back as 1840, appearing as witness before the House of Commons Select Committee on the Health of Towns, he had given evidence as to the deplorable sanitary circumstances of the poorer population of Liverpool; and, later in the same year, he had answered the inquiry of the Poor Law Commissioners by a Report (No. 19 in their subsequently published series of *Local Reports*) on the sanitary state of the labouring classes in the town. At that time he had already for ten years been one of the physicians to the Liverpool Dispensaries; and his evidence and report show at every turn that he was most intimately acquainted with the sanitary conditions of which he spoke, and had long given intelligent and humane consideration to means of improving them. In 1843, he had impressed public opinion in Liverpool by a paper read before the Literary and Philosophical Society of the city, substantially to the effect of the report he had made to the Poor Law Commissioners, on the causes of the high general death-rate at Liverpool—a death-rate which at that time averaged annually about 36 per 1,000 living; and it seems certain that this paper of his was a principal influence in determining the subsequent activity of the Liverpool Corporation. Appointed health-officer for Liverpool in 1847, Dr. Duncan remained in office till 1863, when ill-health and approaching death obliged him to retire. Of his sixteen years' official work, there unfortunately do not exist any published circumstantial records; but that his labours were in the highest degree meritorious, is still a tradition in Liverpool, and was at the time so reputed elsewhere. While, as the first-appointed English Officer of Health, he of course had an essentially novel task, he also, in regard of his place of duty, had more than common administrative difficulties to cope with; and it is believed that he attained every success which under those conditions was possible. With the ungrudging confidence and support of a very public-spirited local authority, he established methods of work, and initiated courses of improvement, which have continued to the present day; and under which the average general death-rate of Liverpool has been reduced by probably at least a fourth part of that which prevailed forty years ago. To his influence especially has been due the abolition (probably now complete) of what in earlier days had been among the worst opprobria of Liverpool; the pestiferous *cul-de-sac* courts, which some 80,000 or 90,000 persons of the working classes then had as their dwelling-places, and the 8,000 cellars which some 30,000 or 40,000 persons were inhabiting.

From the documents available it appears that the relationship between Duncan and the Health Committee was always of a very pleasant and friendly character and that the Committee fully supported him in his routine sanitary work and in his frequent differences of opinion with the Select Vestry and its Medical Relief Committee. His official relations with the other Corporation officials, in particular the Town Clerk, the Borough Engineer and the Head Constable, were always cordial and there is no sign in the correspondence of friction between them at any time. It is fortunate that Newlands, the Borough Engineer, and Duncan, the Medical Officer of Health, co-operated so well together, since neither could have done his work so efficiently without the aid of the other. James Newlands—one of the most able officials ever employed by the Liverpool Corporation[1]—had the more difficult job of the two. But he was dealing with material things with which he was familiar and which were fully within his professional competence, such as sewering, paving and cleansing; while Duncan was called upon to face the intangible realities of outbreaks of epidemic diseases,

---

[1] Newlands died in 1871 and was buried at the Necropolis, West Derby Road.

the nature of which neither he nor the medical profession of that time understood. Apart from lack of
knowledge, Duncan suffered from lack of resources.
The difficulty was not merely office staff but the lack
of hospitals, doctors and nurses under his own control.
All these resources belonged to the two Boards of
Guardians—the Select Vestry and the West Derby
Board of Guardians—and it was at times the Medical
Officer of Health's duty to attempt to persuade these
bodies to make preparations in advance for an impend-
ing epidemic and, during it, to supply hospitals and
doctors according to the size of the outbreak. It is not
in the least surprising that repeated differences of
opinion arose during such epidemics between Duncan
and the Medical Relief Committee of the Select Vestry
on the subject of the scale of the provision to be made
for the unfortunate victims of the disease, and that the
Medical Officer of Health, who was himself seeing
daily in the courts and cellars the hapless sufferers from
cholera or typhus, should press for more hospital
accommodation and more medical visitors than the
Parish Guardians were willing to supply.

For the benefit of any non-medical readers who may
chance to see this book it may be well to give some
account of the present-day arrangements for preventing
epidemics and for dealing with those which occasionally
occur, in spite of the vigilance of the Public Health
Authorities. It has been said that Duncan was handi-
capped by lack of knowledge and lack of resources.
Even the resources of the Boards of Guardians were
pitifully meagre. To-day we are in a much stronger
position in regard to knowledge and resources and are,
in particular, able to prevent the occurrence of most
epidemics of infectious diseases so that, with more
doctors and more hospitals, we have at the worst far
fewer cases to deal with. The reason why it is possible
to-day to prevent many epidemics is found in the dis-
coveries by Pasteur, Koch and others during the last
half of the nineteenth century of the causative organisms

which, gaining admission to the human body in several ways, may produce attacks of specific infectious diseases. In this way, before the end of the century, mankind knew for the first time in its history the origins of some of the more important infectious diseases, such as cholera, typhoid and dysentery, and from this knowledge it was practicable, by appropriate methods, to study the ways in which these diseases were transmitted from one person to another and, in many cases, to prevent their spread.[1] Some of these diseases defied the search for the causative organisms until the twentieth century, e.g. typhus and scarlet fever, but to-day our knowledge of this aspect of the science of bacteriology is nearly complete.

Medical science has, however, gone one step further. Not only are the causative organisms of these diseases known and often destroyed before they can pass from the patient to other persons, but scientists have developed methods of *immunizing* individuals, thereby conferring upon them a large measure of protection against specific communicable diseases. These measures of protection, it should be noted, do not confer absolute immunity on all persons in all circumstances, but they largely increase the resisting power of the individual, rendering him less liable to attack.

Many such methods of immunization against infectious diseases, including all the diseases of this kind which the Medical Officer of Health in the middle of last century had to deal with, are now available and, judiciously used, are a powerful weapon in the hands of the modern sanitarian. Duncan, however, knew of only one weapon of this kind, viz. vaccination against smallpox, and this service was administered by the Boards of Guardians.

In another and equally important way the modern

---

[1] The following are the dates when some of the principal disease-producing organisms were first identified: anthrax, 1849 (Pollender); typhoid, 1880–1 (Eberth); tuberculosis, 1882 (Koch); cholera, 1883 (Koch); diphtheria, 1883 (Klebs); plague, 1894 (Kitasato and Yersin); dysentery, 1898 (Shiga); scarlet fever, 1923 (Dick).

Health Department is better equipped for dealing with outbreaks of the major infectious diseases than was the Medical Officer of Health of a large town a hundred years ago. It has far greater resources of every kind at its command. The most important unit amongst these resources is the local fever hospital to which the early cases in an epidemic—sometimes all the cases—can be sent, with a view to preventing such patients from spreading further the disease. In the epidemics in the fifth and sixth decades of last century the hospital accommodation was in the hands of the Boards of Guardians and it was not until after the Public Health Act, 1875, that it became customary for Town Councils to own fever hospitals. After 1930 in the larger towns of county borough status, through the operation of the Local Government Act, 1929, other types of hospital accommodation besides fever hospitals were in the hands of the local authority or at its disposal, and these were often useful in large epidemics. Moreover, through the operation of the same Act, the Board of Guardians disappeared and their functions in regard to vaccination, registration of death, and other matters had been transferred to local authorities. The modern Medical Officer of Health has therefore great advantages as compared with Dr. Duncan—he has fewer and smaller epidemics because the means of prevention are better; he has a sufficient number of hospital beds at his disposal, and he receives early information about the incidence of infectious diseases in his area through the system of compulsory notification of such diseases to him. He does not have to rely upon house-to-house visitation, as Duncan did, for information as to the number of cases and the districts from which they come. Notifications by medical practitioners to the Medical Officer of Health give promptly all the information necessary as to the course of any epidemic.

In actual fact this country has been singularly free from epidemics of the more serious of the infectious diseases for many years. The spread of knowledge, the improved housing of the people, the greatly increased efficiency of the services of local authorities, especially in regard to sanitation and water supplies, have practically banished from our midst the diseases which gave Duncan most anxiety. Cholera and typhus—except for an occasionally imported case of the latter—have not been seen in this country for several decades, and typhoid, although not yet completely stamped out, seldom reaches epidemic proportions. Scarlet fever, a severe disease in Duncan's day, with a high case mortality, now causes very few deaths and is regarded as one of the minor infectious diseases.

Let us consider some of the improvements which have taken place in public health since Duncan and Newlands, under the supervision of the Town Council's Health Committee, pioneered the work of sanitary improvement in Liverpool a hundred years ago. A century is, of course, a long period of time, and we would expect great advances to have taken place and new fields, unknown to these pioneers in sanitation, to have been opened up. This has, in fact, been the case. During the intervening period much legislation, dealing with the health of the public from every possible angle, has been passed by Parliament. In some decades the rate of advance has been slow; in some—and this especially applies to the period between the two great wars—progress has been rapid. But whether slow or rapid the history of the public health movement in this country, since the middle of last century, has been one of sustained and continuous progress. The Health Committee of 1847, faced with epidemics which they rightly thought arose out of the appalling conditions under which most of the population of the borough lived, strove with the help of their officers to improve the sanitary condition of Liverpool, and in their efforts to this end they achieved a large measure of success. More than that, they perfected an administrative machine which would be used, as the years went by, to effect further improvements. Though the pioneers of those days imperfectly realized it, sanitation was only one of the methods which would be used in time to come to raise the standard of the health of the community to levels undreamed of by them. The poorer people of that day were largely illiterate, intemperate, ill-fed and badly housed. Their lives were indeed nasty, brutish and short. What have been the steps by which a population of this kind has been raised, in the space of a hundred years, to the standards of health and culture enjoyed by the community to-day?

Perhaps the most important of these steps—and there were many of them—were housing, education, personal hygiene, National Health Insurance, and a general improvement in the standard of living. By the end of the nineteenth century the sanitary work of the reformers had been largely completed and Liverpool and the majority of the larger towns had reached relatively satisfactory standards of communal cleanliness. The standards of housing of the people were still disappointingly low, but many of the older narrow courts had disappeared and only a small number of families were living in cellars. Much of the work of condemning the older types of dwelling-houses in Liverpool was performed under the auspices of Dr. E. W. Hope, who was Medical Officer of Health of Liverpool from 1894 to 1924, and whose period of office was signalized by many improvements in the city's public health services, including the introduction of maternity and child welfare, the medical inspection and treatment of children attending elementary schools, and measures for dealing with tuberculosis and venereal diseases. This work of Hope and others, which initiated the personal health services, was of great and lasting importance and, from the pioneering point of view, fully deserves to rank with that of Duncan in the sphere of sanitation.

It has been said that the population of Liverpool during most of last century was largely illiterate; and this illiteracy was not only harmful from the social point of view but also from the health point of view.

An illiterate urban population can never be a healthy population. The extension of the franchise by Lord Beaconsfield in 1867 brought the question of the education of the people into the domain of urgent reforms and in 1870 the first Education Act was passed. An Act of this wide scope required many years before it could be brought fully into operation, but before the end of the century elementary education up to the age of fourteen had become universal and compulsory. Thus, very slowly and very gradually, a literate population was evolved. Moreover, through the educational system, the whole of the child population of this country came under the vigilant eyes of the teachers, who soon began to comment about the clothing, footwear and health conditions generally of their pupils. Comment became criticism and criticism of the health standards of the child populations in our industrial towns was voiced year after year at educational conferences and in the Press. Nevertheless, the initiation of a school medical service was long delayed and it was not until 1907 that legislative provision was made for the medical inspection of children attending elementary schools.[1] Since then improvements and extensions of the school medical service have continued, and to-day this service provides medical inspection and free treatment of all kinds to children attending any type of school under the control of the local education authority.[2]

Assistance to the expectant mother and the infant and young child, as a nation-wide service, came much later and it was not until 1918 that the Maternity and Child Welfare Act empowered local authorities to spend money on the care of these most important classes in the community.

During the years which have passed since the beginning of the present century a mass of legislation has been placed on the Statute Book, having as its aim the conferring of some measure of social security upon the

[1] Education (Administrative Provisions) Act, 1907.
[2] Education Act, 1944.

poorer members of the community. Apart from the
National Health Insurance Act, 1911, there have been
passed Acts of Parliament relating to old-age pensions,
unemployment, blind persons, compensation for acci-
dent, etc., and the provision made thereby has not only
rendered the lot of many people more secure during
times of illness or misfortune but has had the effect
of maintaining a standard of health amongst all classes
of the community which would have astonished our
ancestors of a hundred years ago.

The services discussed in the preceding paragraphs
are usually referred to as the Personal Health Services
while the methods used by the Liverpool Health Committee in Duncan's time are spoken of as Environmental
Health Services. Personal health services such as
maternity and child welfare deal directly with the
individual or, at most, with the family; the environmental health services are *community* services providing
generally for the inhabitants of a street, a district or a
town. The environmental health services such as the
provision of sewers, the paving of streets, the supply
of pure water, the removal and disposal of refuse, etc.,
are fundamental services in the absence of which—as
Liverpool found in the first half of the nineteenth century—it becomes well-nigh impossible for an urban
community to exist at all. Chadwick, Duncan and the
other health reformers of last century were therefore
right in putting first things first and concentrating all
their efforts on sanitation, thereby ensuring the continued existence of the densely populated urban communities for which they were responsible. Efficient
sanitary measures went some distance towards improving the health of the inhabitants of our towns and
as a result of this the mortality statistics markedly
improved and epidemics of cholera and typhoid largely
disappeared. But the virtual suppression of epidemics
and an appreciable reduction in death-rates only went a
short way towards the solution of the problem of
ensuring and maintaining the health of the population.

Much still remained to be accomplished while the greater part of the working-class population was ill-housed, poorly fed and illiterate. Evidently there was no single avenue of approach to the problem of improving the mental and physical health of all the members of the community. The solution was to be found in many diverse directions—in sanitation, housing, education, the personal health services, hospitals, social security, economics, and in many other ways, some of which have only been understood during the past decade. Modern communities are attacking the problem of improving the physical and mental health of the people by these and other methods and much success has attended their efforts.

Faced with urgent and critical issues the reformers of the nineteenth century tackled immediate problems and within a period of two decades they had laid the foundations on which the Public Health Services of our day were to be built. And what immense foundations they were! They involved the great engineering feats of sewering, draining, and paving a very large town and (in the case of Liverpool) of bringing water supplies to it first from Rivington and then from Vyrnwy, seventy miles away. Similar schemes were carried out by other large towns. The success of these measures is not to be assessed in terms of death-rates alone. They must also be considered from the point of view of health, comfort and amenity. From the standpoint of mortality the sanitary improvements initiated by the Liverpool Health Committee in 1847 had the effect of reducing the average death-rate of the town from about 35 per 1,000 of the population to 25 by the end of the century, chiefly by preventing the occurrence of serious epidemics of the principal zymotic diseases. How far the town had still to go in devising further measures for the improvement of the health of the community may be shown by considering infantile mortality rates—a sensitive index of the social and health standards of any area. Even as late as 1895 the infantile mortality rate in Liverpool stood at the abnormally high figure of 202 per 1,000 children born, although this was better than it had been earlier in the century. To-day, largely because of the provision made for the care of the expectant mother and the infant, this rate in Liverpool had gone down to 45, and may confidently be expected to become still more favourable.

One of the most important lessons which the pioneers in sanitation who lived in the first half of last century taught their day and generation was the fact that the community as a whole has inescapable responsibilities for some part of the welfare of each unit in it. As time went on this sense of corporate responsibility pervaded more and more the life of the nation until its culmination, during the later years of the war we have just passed through, in the ideas of a National Insurance and National Health Service. Such comprehensive and all-embracing schemes were remote from the minds of Chadwick, Farr, Duncan and Newlands a hundred years ago; but out of the seeds sown by them with such infinite labour and patience in the early days of the reign of Queen Victoria there has grown a system of health and social services which, with all its faults and deficiencies, is a credit to the nation which brought it forth.

INDEX

A

Abercromby Square, 50
Acts of Parliament
  Baths and Wash-houses Act, 1846, 107
  Education Act, 1870, 157
  Education Act, 1944, 157
  Education (Administrative Provisions) Act, 1907, 157
  Liverpool Building Act, 1842, 21, 30, 34, 35, 41, 44, 89
  Liverpool Improvement Act, 1842, 15, 34
  Liverpool Sanitary Act, 1846, 21, 22, 33, 35, 39, 43, 45, 50, 56, 80, 88, 89, 105, 108
  Liverpool Sanitary Amendment Act, 1854, 43, 90
  Local Government Act, 1929, 136, 154
  Maternity and Child Welfare Act, 1918, 157
  Municipal Corporations Act, 1835, 21
  National Health Insurance Act, 1911, 158
  National Health Service Act, 1946, 136
  Nuisances Removal and Diseases Prevention Act, 1848, 108
  Nuisances Removal and Diseases Prevention Amendment Act, 1849, 108
  Poor Law Amendment Act, 1834, 31
  Public Health Act, 1848, 33, 43
  Public Health Act, 1875, 154
  Vaccination Acts, 1867–1907, 136
Ansdell Street Temporary Hospital, 69
Athenaeum Library, Liverpool, 7

B

Baines's *History of Liverpool*, 48
Baths and wash-houses, 107, 124, 131, 136
Beaconsfield, Earl of, 157
Bentham, Jeremy, 30
Bickerton, T. H., 49
Birmingham, 29
Bradley, Edward, 81
Brétonneau, 99
Bridewells, 140–1
Buccleuch, Duke of, 33

C

Cameron, Dr., 91, 144
Cardwell, Edward (Viscount Cardwell), 136
Carlyle, Thomas, 17
Chadwick, Sir Edwin, 11, 12, 17, 30, 31, 39, 112, 115, 158, 160
Cholera, 121, 122
Cholera epidemics, 49, 63–5, 68, 79–89, 91–6
"Clare Wheeler," 123
Commission of Inquiry into the State of Large Towns and Populous Districts, 37
Common day schools, 28
Currie, Dr., 77, 116
Currie, Rev. James, 12

D

Dame schools, 28
Diarrhoea and dysentery, 56, 58, 69
Diphtheria, 99
Dumfries, 72
Duncan, George, 12
Duncan, William Henry
  Appointed M.O.H., 45, 46; birth, 12; cellar dwellings, 77–8; cholera epidemics, 49,

161